THROUGHOUT THE AGES, METAPHYSICAL
TRADITIONS HAVE BEEN TRANSLATED
INTO SACRED AND VISIONARY ART.
THE LIBRARY OF ESOTERICA
EXPLORES THE SYMBOLIC LANGUAGE
OF OUR MOST POTENT UNIVERSAL
STORIES, THE TALES WE TELL THROUGH
PAINT AND INK, COSTUME AND CLAY.

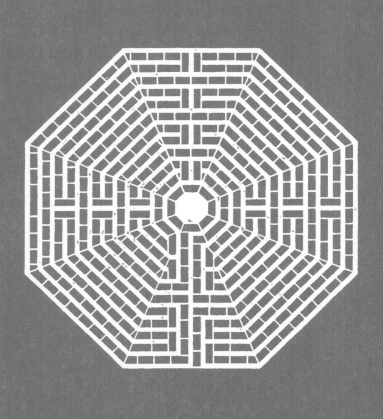

THE LIBRARY
OF
ESOTERICA

SACRED SITES

FOREWORD BY
Lita Albuquerque

DESIGN BY
Thunderwing

EDITED BY
Jessica Hundley

TASCHEN

SACRED SITES

Foreword by
LITA ALBUQUERQUE

EARTH MAPPING

Just as we wish to pursue a pleasant object that moves away from us we enjoy gazing upon blue—not because it forces itself upon us, but because it draws us after it.

— JOHANN WOLFGANG VON GOETHE, Author & Poet, from *Theory of Colour*, 1810

(frontispiece) William Henry Matthews · *Mazes and Labyrinths* **· United States · 1922** One of the many photographed documentations from Henry's 1922 book, *Mazes and Labyrinths; A General Account of Their History and Developments*, which explores the origins of ancient sites, mazes, and labyrinths around the globe.

When humans first landed on the moon, I was twenty-two years old, and we had never before seen an image of the Earth from space. That first photograph of our home planet was a seminal moment for my generation. I started having visions of mapping the stars, here on the Earth. As an artist, eventually I made a commitment that my work was going to be about the relationship between the earth and the sky. I started doing projects out in the environment that were about placing objects on the ground in relation to the horizon line or to the mountains or to the moon, and the stars. Geography, location, and the land all became very important parts in the conceptualization of my projects. My intention in my work is precisely to anchor a specific place and a certain moment in time. Where the work is located is important, not only for anchoring, but also for the work's aesthetic. The environment where a piece is located is an integral part that showcases the interrelationship (and interdependence) of the viewer, with the environment. We are always completely connected to what is around us.

I decided, early in my career to claim the relationship between the Earth and the sky.

I picked the color ultramarine to unite the two because of the intensity of the color— it had a certain vibration to it. I was raised in Tunisia, North Africa, famous for its ultramarine doors and windows on the whitewashed buildings. That blue against the white made an imprint on my mind. In the mid-1970s I started doing works out in the landscape and they were all with this blue, which for me was a way of uniting the earth and the sky.

My core interest is always to be conscious of where the planet and the body are located, in space-time. In early 2000's I began to create a character within my works, a "25th century female astronaut." She is symbol, a stand-in for us today and a guide toward where we need to be. She represents interstellar consciousness. We are related to the stars, connected to them. To be fluent in the language between earth and sky, between body and space, is to understand that connection and how that partnership opens the body up to the sublime.

— Lita Albuquerque
Artist & Scholar
Los Angeles, 2024

Lita Albuquerque · *NAJMA Returns* **· United States 2021** From a film still created in collaboration between Albuquerque, Hesham Alsaifi, and Nicole McDonald, *NAJMA* is a continuation of Albuquerque's projects in one of the great deserts of the world. For the artist, deserts are places to listen and connect to the rich history of celestial traditions.

Preface by
JESSICA HUNDLEY

A SACRED STATE

What is sacred? Of what is the spirit made? What is worth living for and what is worth dying for? The answer to each is the same. Only love.

— LORD BYRON, from the epic poem of *Don Juan*, 1824

Through gathering, we ignite our spaces with spirit, we circle the bonfire, bow down at the forest altar, give praise at the temple to our chosen divinities. Through pilgrimage, we carve indelible pathways, making our meditative way across continents, generations of footsteps treading, again and again, upon sacred grounds. And through our creative offerings we envision new worlds, wildly imaginative odes to what we deem as holy; golden temples hewn of rock, enormous spirals sculpted from sand and soil, silent sanctuaries hidden among wooded groves. We paint the ancient cave walls, carve petroglyphs to mark the way, place roses in veneration at the candlelit altar.

Slowly, stone-by-stone, we build monuments to our gods, a cosmic geometry held within our sacred architecture of worship. These hidden patterns can be found in the mysterious, towering pyramids seen across the globe and throughout an astounding diversity of cultures, in the marble sanctuaries built to house the Greek and Roman goddesses, and in the windblown mountain monasteries of

ancient Asia and the indigenous cliff-dwellings of the American Southwest. Nature, art, beauty, these are the common elements found, both within the places made sacred by our ancestors and in the multitude of environments where we strive to connect to both to source, and to ourselves.

Tracing a hallowed route from rugged stone temples to transcendent works of modern architecture, this volume of our ongoing series celebrates the collective history of spaces made sacrosanct through human worship. We explore the history of sacred art and architecture, showcasing the myriads of ways in which we imbue our environments with profound and enduring meaning. From our early designation of nature and the body as temple and to our futuristic embrace of imaginary realms, as humans and as seekers, we continue to travel the vast and mystical landscapes of myth, religion, and imagination.

— Jessica Hundley
Series Editor
Los Angeles, 2024

Annie Besant and Charles Leadbeater · *The Music of Gounod* · **England** · **1901** From the radical book *Thought Forms*, by the theosophical duo Besant and Leadbetter, on how our thoughts manifest as auric waves—visible to those with the physic skills to see them, is an illustration of Charles Gounod's music funneling out of a cathedral in colored phenomena.

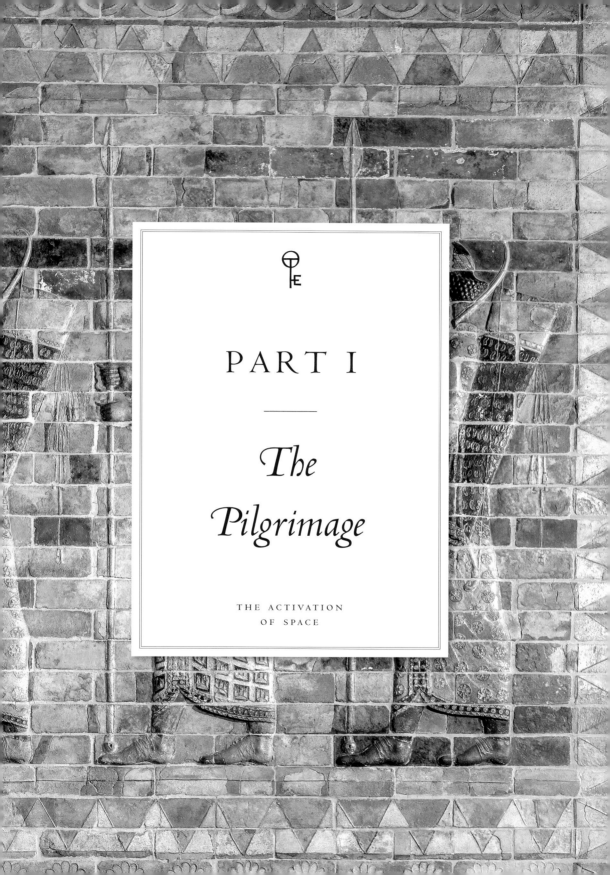

PART I

The

Pilgrimage

THE ACTIVATION
OF SPACE

THE JOURNEY BEGINS

A Brief History of People and Places

Some form of common worship and a common place of worship, appear to be a human necessity.
— MAHATMA GANDHI, Lawyer, Activist & Pacifist, from his writings, 1925

We worship first at the altar of the womb, emerging into the world through the portal of the feminine and evolving through the nurturing of our Great Mother, the Earth. The first humans created sacred spaces within the smoke-stained cathedrals of the caverns and caves in which they found shelter and in the verdant groves of fruit trees and in the vast expanse of desert sands.

They discovered the divine within nature, in the movement of both the stars above and of their own bodies below, arms raised in praise, feet tracing the patterns of ancient dances. The first temples were constructed of carved primordial stones, the first sacraments gifted within the circle of bodies gathering around a fire. The elements themselves were our gods and goddesses—the fertile earth, the tempestuous skies, the flow of river and ocean and the flames which warmed our skin.

Throughout human history, sacred sites have held profound significance and importance

for various cultures around the world. These sites, imbued with spiritual, cultural, and historical resonance, serve as points of connection between humanity and the divine, the natural world and the cosmos. These spaces hold tremendous importance, serving as physical manifestations of spiritual beliefs and cultural values. From ancient temples and burial grounds to the paths crossed by the devout in pilgrimage, sacred sites have played a vital role in shaping the beliefs, practices, and identities of diverse civilizations.

The latter is one of the key reasons why sacred sites remain vitally important, as they serve as enduring repositories of cultural heritage and history. Many sacred places around the globe have been designated as UNESCO World Heritage Sites due to their significance in conveying the shared heritage of humanity. These sites are often home to monuments and artifacts that provide valuable insights into the beliefs and rituals of

(previous pages) Unknown · *Frieze of Archers, Susa* Iran · 6th Century BCE Made from bricks of siliceous clay, the procession of warrior-archers panel is from the exquisite Palace of Darius the Great from the ancient Iranian Achaemenid Period, spared from Alexander the Great's destruction of Persepolis.

Myriam Wares · *A Quiet Stroll in Time* · Canada 2021–22 One half of a surrealist diptych by Wares, the self-taught illustrator invites the viewer to contemplate the passage of time within a grand labyrinth.

past civilizations. For example, the Pyramids of Giza in Egypt, Stonehenge in England, and Machu Picchu in Peru, are all sacred sites considered iconic symbols of human ingenuity and spiritual expression.

Located in Wiltshire, England, Stonehenge is perhaps one of the most iconic prehistoric monuments in the world. Constructed around 2500 BCE, this Neolithic site consists of large standing stones arranged in a circular pattern. While its purpose remains a subject of debate, it is widely believed to have held religious or ceremonial significance. The stones, some weighing up to 25 tons, were quarried and transported from a considerable distance, indicating the

immense effort invested in the construction. The alignment of the stones with celestial events, such as the summer solstice, suggests that Stonehenge served as an observatory and a place of celestial worship. In Ireland, Newgrange is another important ancient site, a passage tomb built around 3200 BCE, making it older than both Stonehenge and the Great Pyramids of Egypt. The tomb's main chamber is aligned with the winter solstice sunrise. Newgrange's construction required advanced engineering techniques and a deep understanding of astronomy. The elaborate stone carvings found within the tomb depicts spirals, circles, and other symbols, suggesting a complex belief system. The site's alignment with celestial

Unknown · *Dream Stele* · Egypt · ca. 1400 BCE The carved granite dream stele situated between the paws of the Great Sphinx commemorates the dream vision of Prince Thutmose IV. Thutmose's eventual rulership served to change the course of Egyptian history.

Unknown · *Pyramids of Cheops, Kafre, and Menkaura* Egypt · 19th Century A watercolor painting of the pyramids, built to house the Ka or soul of the pharaohs in the afterlife, depicts a verdant landscape along a branch of the Nile River that once flowed near the sacred Giza Valley.

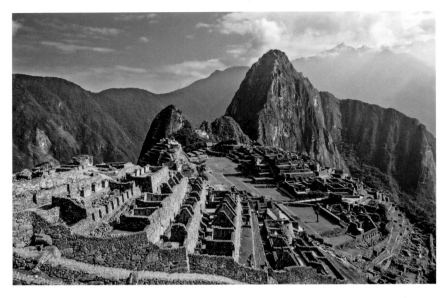

events and its intricate artwork indicates a profound connection between prehistoric people and the cycles of nature. Göbekli Tepe, located in southeastern Turkey, dates to approximately 9600 BCE, predating Stonehenge by several millennia. This site consists of massive stone pillars arranged in circular structures, depicting intricately carved animals and symbols. Its purpose, like Stonehenge, is thought to be religious or ceremonial. The site's age suggests that prehistoric societies were capable of organizing large-scale communal efforts for building such monumental structures, contradicting previous assumptions about our hunter-gatherer ancestors. Also located in England, is the town of Glastonbury, a place known for both it's historical and mystical significance. Believed to be the site of the mythical Isle of Avalon, the final resting place of King

Arthur, Glastonbury is also home to the Glastonbury Abbey, an important medieval monastery. The area is thought to have been a center of pagan worship before the arrival of Christianity and remains a popular destination for spiritual seekers.

Ancient Egypt, with its deep connection to the spiritual realm, is home to some of the most important sacred sites in the world. One of the most famous and enduring is the Great Pyramid of Giza, an architectural marvel that has fascinated and perplexed scholars, archaeologists, and visitors for centuries. Built during the Fourth Dynasty of the Old Kingdom, around 2580-2560 BCE, the Great Pyramid is the largest and most well-known of the three pyramids at Giza, serving as the tomb of Pharaoh Khufu. Its colossal size, precise engineering, and astronomical

Unknown · *Machu Picchu* · Peru · 15th Century Majestically overlooking the sacred valley below sits the palatial Incan ruins, a spiritually significant city built with astrological architecture upon an x-shaped fault line, with impeccable and mysterious skill.

Lesser Ury · *Moses (approaching Mt. Sinai)* · Germany 1905—07 Moses ascends Mt. Sinai to commune with God, who came down in a thunderous fire cloud, resulting in the Ten Commandments. Ury interprets Moses' journey to the fiery mountaintop in his unique impressionistic technique.

alignment has led to numerous theories and speculations about its purpose, construction methods, and symbolic significance. The Great Pyramid, along with its neighboring pyramids of Khafre and Menkaure, represents the pinnacle of ancient Egyptian funerary architecture and religious belief, reflecting the Pharaoh's quest for immortality and divine kingship in the afterlife.

The temple complex of Karnak, located near the modern city of Luxor is another Egyptian sacred site, constructed over a period of more than 2,000 years from the Middle Kingdom to the Ptolemaic period. Karnak is one of the largest temple complexes in Egypt, dedicated to the god Amun-Ra, the king of the gods. Karnak served as a center of religious worship, ritual, and pilgrimage, attracting devotees from across the kingdom who came to pay homage to the gods, seek divine guidance,

and participate in elaborate festivals and ceremonies. The Valley of the Kings, located on the west bank of the Nile River near Luxor is also renowned for its royal tombs and funerary artifacts. The valley served as a burial ground for the Pharaohs and high-ranking officials of the New Kingdom, from the 16th to the 11th centuries BCE, and is home to tombs of famous Pharaohs such as Tutankhamun, Ramses II, Seti I, and Hatshepsut. These tombs were adorned with intricate murals, hieroglyphs, and funerary objects that were meant to accompany the Pharaoh in the afterlife and ensure their journey to the realm of the gods. The Great Sphinx of Giza is another of the ancient Egyptian masterworks, a massive statue of a creature with the body of a lion and the head of a pharaoh, believed to represent the ruler Khafre. It is located near the Great Pyramids on the Giza Plateau in Egypt and is one of the most famous and iconic

Unknown · *Mayan Pyramid in Chichen Itza* · Mexico 900–1000 The Kukulkan temple sits at a cross between four cenotes. During the equinox, the sun casts a feathered serpent shadow appearing to slither down the mathematically perfected steps, terminating at a carved limestone snake head.

Unknown · *Stonehenge, Winter Solstice* · England ca. 2500 BCE Like many ancient sacred structures built with adept cosmic knowledge, Stonehenge was mysteriously erected and aligns with the sun on solstices.

monuments in the world. The Sphinx is believed to have been built during the reign of Pharaoh Khafre in the 26th century BCE and is thought to have served as a guardian of the pyramids, serving as a symbol of royal power and protection.

The pyramids constructed in the ancient city of Teotihuacan in Mexico are another important sacred space showcasing the spiritual and cultural practices of the Mesoamerican civilizations. Teotihuacan, meaning "the place where the gods were created," in the Nahuatl language, is home to the Pyramid of the Sun, the Pyramid of the Moon, and the Temple of the Feathered Serpent, iconic structures that served as ceremonial and ritual centers for the Aztecs, Maya, and other indigenous peoples. The

city's layout, architecture, and art reflect a deep reverence for the cosmos, nature, and the supernatural forces that were believed to govern human life and destiny.

Chichen Itza, located in the Yucatan Peninsula of Mexico, was once a thriving metropolis of the Mayan civilization and features the towering pyramid known as El Castillo, or the Temple of Kukulkan. Rising 79 feet high, the pyramid is a testament to the mathematical and astronomical knowledge of the Mayans. Aligned with the movements of the sun, the site offers a stunning visual display during the spring and fall equinoxes, when the shadow of a serpent seems to slither down the side of the steps. In addition to the Temple of Kukulkan, Chichen Itza is home to several other remarkable structures, such as the Great Ball Court, the Temple of the Warriors, and the Group of a Thousand Columns. One of the most intriguing aspects of Chichen Itza is the Sacred Cenote, a large natural sinkhole that was used by the Mayans for sacrificial offerings. The discovery of human remains and artifacts in the cenote has shed light on the religious practices of the Mayan people and their reverence for water as a sacred element.

To the south, high in the Peruvian Andes, Machu Picchu still stands as a testament to the ingenuity, spirituality, and architectural prowess of the ancient Inca civilization. This iconic archaeological site, perched on a steep ridge overlooking the Urubamba River valley, draws visitors from around the world. Machu Picchu, meaning "Old Mountain" in

Unknown · *The Wailing Wall or Western Wall* Jerusalem · ca. 19 BCE Built by King Herod, the only remaining wall from the holy Jewish temple on Mount Moriah, second to the temple built by King Solomon, is said to have been that which housed the Ark of the Covenant.

Ra Paulette · *Tree of Life Cave* · United States 2011–19 Artist Ra Paulette hand-carved 14 subterranean caves in the northern New Mexico desert, painstakingly chiseling his works from the organic forms already present in these underground chambers.

Quechua, was built by the Inca Emperor Pachacuti in the 15th century as a royal estate and ceremonial center. Situated at an elevation of over 7,000 feet above sea level, the layout of Machu Picchu is characterized by a series of interconnected plazas, temples, palaces, and residential buildings, showcasing the Inca's sophisticated knowledge of urban planning, engineering, and celestial alignment. The precision and craftsmanship of the stone masonry, the intricate carvings and niches, and the strategic orientation of the structures all reflect the Inca's reverence for nature, the cosmos, and the divine order of the universe.

One of the most iconic features of Machu Picchu is the Intihuatana, or "Hitching Post of the Sun," a massive stone pillar located in the center of the site that served as an astronomical observatory. The Intihuatana is believed to have been used by the Inca priests to track the movements of the sun, moon, and stars, aligning their rituals and agricultural practices with the cycles of nature and the celestial calendar. The concept of the Intihuatana reflects the Inca's profound connection to the cosmos and their belief in the interconnectedness of all life, energy, and consciousness, highlighting their spiritual wisdom and reverence for the natural world.

Across the globe, in India, Varanasi, the ancient city located on the banks of the Ganges River, is considered one of the holiest cities in Hinduism, and a major pilgrimage destination for millions of devotees who come to bathe in the sacred river,

Hasui Kawase · *Clearing After a Snowfall on Mt. Fuji (Tagonoura Beach)* · Japan · 1932 Japanese indigenous people, the Ainu, venerated Mt. Fuji as a portal to the otherworld. Kawase made 52 different woodblock prints of the sacred mountain.

Unknown · *Threshold stone from Newgrange* · Ireland ca. 3200 BCE The ancient temple of Newgrange in East Ireland, known as a passage tomb, was built to align with the rising sun on the winter solstice. The entrance, or kerbstone, is carved with megalithic markings.

cremate their loved ones, and seek spiritual purification. The city's ghats, or riverside steps, are lined with temples, shrines, and ashrams, creating a vibrant hub of spiritual practice, ritual, and devotion. Varanasi's mystical aura and profound connection to life, death, and rebirth have inspired generations of poets, mystics, and seekers. The valley of Kathmandu in Nepal is another important site that holds immense cultural, historical, and spiritual significance, home to ancient temples, stupas, and palaces that are considered sacred by Hindus, Buddhists, and other religious communities. The valley's rich architectural and artistic heritage reflects a blend of Hindu and Buddhist traditions, with sites such as the Pashupatinath Temple, Boudhanath Stupa, and Swayambhunath Stupa serving as focal points of pilgrimage, worship, and meditation.

In North America, the revered sacred site of Chaco Canyon in New Mexico was the center of the ancestral Pueblo culture and is home to numerous ancient ruins, including the famous Pueblo Bonito. The canyon is believed to be a place of great spiritual power, where ceremonies, rituals, and astronomical observations were conducted. Bear Butte in South Dakota, known as "Mato Paha" in Lakota, is a towering igneous rock formation that is considered a sacred mountain by several Plains tribes, including the Lakota, Cheyenne, and Arapaho. It is a place of prayer, vision quests, and ceremonies. Many believe that Bear Butte is a place where the spirits of their ancestors reside, and where they can communicate with the Great Spirit.

These are just a few examples of the innumerable sacred spaces around the globe, each with its own unique history and significance. Whether it is a plant medicine ceremony in the Amazonian jungle, prayers left at the Wailing Wall or walking the meditative

Unknown · *Pueblo Indian cliff dwellings* · United States · ca. 12th Century The most famous of the Mesa Verde National Park, Colorado cliff dwellings is Cliff Palace, with over one hundred fifty rooms and twenty ritual kiva rooms.

James Jacques Joseph Tissot · *The Seven Trumpets of Jericho* · France · 1902 After receiving a religious vision, Tissot spent his later life painting biblical events. With the *Ark of the Covenant* in tow, the Israelites follow God's instruction that seven priests, with seven horns, circle Jericho for seven days.

labyrinth at the Chartres Cathedral, each of these spaces and rituals hold a powerful sense of spirituality and connection to the divine. These sites have the power to transcend borders and bring people together in shared reverence. They serve as reminders of the interconnectedness of humanity and the universal quest for meaning and purpose. These sites also often serve as catalysts for intercultural dialogue, understanding, and cooperation among diverse communities. Many sacred sites are shared by multiple religious and cultural groups, who come together to worship, celebrate, and pay homage. These encounters often lead to cross-cultural exchanges, mutual respect, and a deepening sense of interconnectedness among people of different backgrounds, beliefs, and faiths.

Unknown · *Winged, Human-headed Bull* · Iraq
9th Century BCE Alabaster Lamassu stood guard at ancient Assyrian doorways. Considered celestial beings in Mesopotamia, they bore a human head, symbolizing intelligence; a bull body, symbolizing strength; and eagle wings to symbolize freedom.

Anonymous · *Ganga, The Sacred River* · India
1803–04 Ganga is the personification of the River Ganges, who rides a crocodile and is esteemed as the Mother of all humanity. Sacred Ganges water bestows blessings and cleanses on all who bathe in her, having descended from the heavens to earth.

These spaces also serve as bridges between the past and the present, the material and the spiritual, and the individual and the collective. They remind us of our ancestry, our genetic roots linking us to the ancient rites and rituals of the past, to our connection to the land, the skies, to fire, water, air, and soil. The most sacred place of all, of course, is Earth. Divinity can be found in the reverence we hold for both our planet and own bodies, minds, and actions. Nature is sacrosanct—the oceans, the mountains, the jagged cave walls—and so in turn is creativity, art, dance, theater, film—all things manifested from the sacred space we create inside ourselves. As the scholar and mythologist Joseph Campbell explained in

his 1995 book, *Reflections on the Art of Living*, "Your sacred space is where you can find yourself again and again. You really don't have a sacred space, a rescue land, until you find somewhere to be that's not a wasteland, some field of action where there is a spring of ambrosia—a joy that comes from inside, not something external that puts joy into you—a place that lets you experience your own will and your own intention and your own wish so that, in small, the Kingdom is there. I think everybody, whether they know it or not, is in need of such a place."

Unknown · *Pech Merle cave* · France · 25,000–16,000 BCE Known as the Dappled Horses, the spotted cave paintings in the Pyrenees mountains of France organically follow the curvature of the rock. The spots are thought to have a transcendental significance, and along with the other animal paintings of Pech Merle, may have been trance-induced through shamanic ritual.

(following) Unknown *Chac-Mool* · Mexico 1185–987 BCE Within the Mayan city of Chichen Itza, Chacmool sculptures were found around temples and other worship spaces and used as sacrificial offering tables. Examples of the reclined figures are found in many Mesoamerican ritual cultures.

Unknown · *Minaret of Jam* · Afghanistan · 12th Century Ghurid sultans of a short-lived medieval, nomadic empire, commissioned the two-hundred-foot tower in the mountains of western Afghanistan.

It served as their summer capital and is covered with verses from the Koran in tile and geometric baked brick designs. It is thought to be a symbol of victory.

THE ENERGETIC
ATLAS
Ley Lines, Vortexes, and Cosmic Geometry

The history of life on earth has been a history of interaction between living things and their surroundings.

— RACHEL CARSON, Author & Environmentalist—from *The Silent Spring*, 1962

If the cosmos is comprised of energy, then the presence of ley lines and vortexes within the Earth itself seems entirely viable—locations of energetic significance tracing throughout various parts of the globe, connecting sites of spiritual import. Hypothetical alignments of ancient and sacred sites, natural landmarks, and prehistoric structures, ley lines are thought by many to have spiritual or mystical significance. Some people believe that ley lines are in fact channels of energy that crisscross the earth and connect various sacred or significant places. Advocates of ley lines suggest that they can be detected using dowsing or other divination techniques.

The initial concept of ley lines was first put forth by English photographer and naturalist Alfred Watkins, who presented the idea to the Naturalist Field Club in his home of Hereford in 1921. Watkins would later go on to pen the book *Early British Trackways* in 1922 and *The Old Straight Track* in 1925, both tomes

developing his theory that various straight lines crisscrossed throughout England, these lines having existed, according to Watkin's thesis, as far back as the Neolithic-era. Watkins also proposed that ancient civilizations may have built their monuments and structures along these invisible lines.

Watkin's ideas were later expanded upon in John Michell's, *The New View Over Atlantis*, first published in 1969. Michell suggested that these ley lines may in fact have mysterious, mystical origins, a concept that eventually become hugely popularized with the advent of the New Age Movement of the 1980s. In his book, Michell gives credence to Watkin's theory and suggests that ley lines might in fact be something far more magickal than even Watkin's himself may have guessed. Michell writes, "Watkins saw straight through the surface of the landscape to a layer deposited in some remote prehistoric age. The barrier of time melted and spread across the country, he

Harold Fisk · *Meander Maps of the Mississippi River* United States · 1944 Fisk both imagines the prehistoric and explores the traceable memory of a river as it forged its own path through thousands of years of changes. Through evolution, human, and nonhuman shifts, the colors represent the passage of time and stages of the river's life.

PLATE 22
SHEET 6

GEOLOGICAL INVESTIGATION
MISSISSIPPI RIVER ALLUVIAL VALLEY
ANCIENT COURSES
MISSISSIPPI RIVER MEANDER BELT
CAPE GIRARDEAU, MO.-DONALDSONVILLE, LA.

IN 15 SHEETS | SCALE IN MILES | SHEET 6

OFFICE OF THE PRESIDENT, MISSISSIPPI RIVER COMMISSION
VICKSBURG, MISS. 1944

TO ACCOMPANY REPORT OF HAROLD N. FISK PH.D. CONSULTANT
LOUISIANA STATE UNIVERSITY, BATON ROUGE, LA., DATED 1 DEC. 1944

R. H. S. - H. N. F. | FILE NO. MRC/2586 SH 33 F

BANKLINE SYMBOLS

Traceable prehistoric final bankline positions of
meanders and mapped historical banklines.

Arbitrarily selected traceable prehistoric bankline
positions marking stages of meander growth.

Indefinite prehistoric bankline positions.

CUT-OFF SYMBOLS

Neck cut-off following indicated stage.

Chute cut-off following indicated stage.

Fault

saw a web of lines linking the holy places and sites of antiquity...In one moment of transcendental perception Watkins entered a magic world of prehistoric Britain, a world whose very existence had been forgotten."

While Michell suggests the existence of a spiritually energetic aspect of the ley line, others believe that they are in fact manmade, either roads by built by Roman invaders in England or established even earlier—ancient

paths carved over time, marking routes of travel and trade. Whether a human-constructed, spiritual, or natural phenomenon, ley lines and vortexes continue to be the subject of intense fascination, believed by many in the esoteric community to be invisible lines or areas of concentrated energy that crisscross the entire world.

In Watkins' homeland of England, the iconic prehistoric monument of Stonehenge is thought to have been built upon one of

Unknown · *Ram Yantra at Jantar Mantar, Delhi* India · 1724 For as long as people have observed the celestial bodies, they've built earth structures to plot their courses. The architectural monument constructed by Raj Jai Singh in 1724 can determine your zodiac sign.

Mohammadreza Domiriganji · *Ceiling of Vakil Mosque, Shiraz* · United Arab Emirates · 2014 The tiled, kaleidoscopic geometry of mosque ceilings use precise, mathematical equations to invoke non-representational nature. Beyond beautiful, the ancient patterns invoke the presence of pure spirit.

the most famous of these global ley lines. Comprised of a circle of giant standing rocks, some theorize that the lines connecting each of the stones forms a powerful segment of the earth's energy grid—expanding outward from Stonehenge toward other sacred sites, some as far flung as Egypt and South America. Stonehenge is said to be a gateway to the otherworld, and its ley lines are often associated with heightened spiritual energies. Glastonbury Tor, also in England, is a hill that is believed to have been a site of spiritual significance for thousands of years. Glastonbury is said to exist on a ley line that connects several other sacred sites in the region, including Stonehenge. Many believe that ancient spiritual monuments around the globe can be traced to these same ley lines that are said to cross over England.

Machu Picchu, for instance, the ancient Incan city of Peru, is thought to also be located upon a ley line that connects the earth to sky. This same ley line is thought to be connected energetically to the Pyramids of Giza, in Egypt. The ancient Incas are said to have used "spirit-lines" or ceques with the Inca Temple of the Sun in Cuzco as their center, the lines marking roads leading to sites of spiritual significance.

In North America, the southwest area of Sedona, Arizona is a site of New Age pilgrimages, with many convinced the location is situated on a particularly powerful vortex. Sedona is surrounded by towering red rock formations, stone towers also thought to emit powerful energetic fields. On the

UNESCO · *Aerial view of Stonehenge* · England 1986 The famed ancient standing stones viewed from above give a glimpse of how the original design could calculate and align with cosmic events.

Unknown · *Paharpur Buddhist Monastery* · Bangladesh 8th Century Shaped as a mandala, a symbol of the creation of the universe with its four directions, this complicated and stellar feat of architectural brilliance is shown from an aerial view.

Western edge of North America, Mount Shasta is also believed to be an energy vortex and sacred site. The mountain is home to numerous legends and stories, with some of area's indigenous tribes believing it to be a place of immense spiritual significance.

The idea of spiritual and mythological pathways can be seen in numerous cultures, from the Irish "fairy paths" to the Chinese "dragon lines." "Songlines," also called "dreaming tracks," are paths across land and sky long recorded by the Australian Aboriginal people in songs, stories, and paintings. The energy of the land itself, is part of what makes sacred sites powerful, alongside the power of mathematics, of cosmic geometry—whether from the mysteries of the labyrinth or the sacred shape of the mandala, all of these elements

come into profound play within the world's religious and spiritual architecture.

Often these geometrically significant symbols, the labyrinth for instance, provide space for moving meditation or for contemplation of spirit. Regardless of tradition or practice, the hand of the gods is said to appear within the details of sacred art and architecture, as seen in the creation of murals, mandalas, and other symbols, art an alchemical process, the transmutation of worship into creative form. Religious and spiritual spaces around the world and through disparate cultures often showcase mathematical, astronomical, or energetic alignment—whether due to position of church cornerstone, or a site's relationship to spin of the earth and the movements of the planets above.

Unknown · *Tao symbol from Qingyang Gong (Green Goat Temple)* · China · 19th Century Said to be the birthplace of Taoism and Lao Zu, the Qingyang Gong Shi is a palace originally built in the Tang Dynasty, ninth century, and rebuilt many times over.

Unknown · *Thangka of Hayagriva mandala* · Tibet 19th Century Avalokiteshvara, the Bodhisattva of compassion in the Tibetan pantheon, is depicted in wrathful form as a protector and destroyer of evil spirits. The surrounding deities and symbology protect from disease, calamity, and negative energy.

Alfred Watkins
Sacrificial Stone · England
1925 Originator of
the idea of ley lines,
Watkins recreates a
scene based on sun
alignments in Greek
and Egyptian temples.
Lines of invisible earth
energy and sun cycles,
known by the ancients,
dictated the placement
of temples, burial
sites, and as the photo
exhibits, sacred
sacrificial grounds.

Buckminster Fuller · *Building Construction / Geodesic
Dome* · United States · 1951 The sacred geometry
of the spherical structure mimicking the fundamental shape of creation, designed by genius polymath
Fuller, is aesthetically captivating even in its blue-
print form.

Daniel Martin Diaz · *Pyramid Frequencies* · United
States · 2021 As the artist explains, "Early civilizations employed arcane methods to tap into harmonic
frequencies to construct monuments and shift colossal structures."

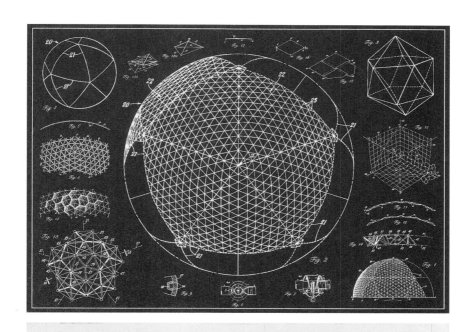

(following, left)
Alexander Graham Bell
Tetrahedral Kites
Scotland/Canada
1903 In addition to
inventing the telephone,
Bell also dabbled in
aerodynamics, design-
ing a series of kites
using pyramid-shaped
cells due to their
geometric structure,
with the ultimate plan
of human flight.

(following, right)
Unknown · *Drawing
from an untitled
manuscript* · Germany
16th Century Held
at the Herzog August
Bibliothek archives, this
illustrated manuscript
showcases the German
Renaissance fascination
for geometrical shapes
as demonstrated by the
likes of Albrecht Dürer
and Johannes Kepler.

Nadia Waheed · *Pilgrims, Sojourners* · United States
2021 Speaking to the conflict between honoring the
past and the homogenization of the modern world,
the artist explores women connecting to ancestral
ways and lands, in an effort, as she explains of,
"trying to find truth or trying to receive truth."

Antoni Gaudí · *The ceiling of the nave in La Sagrada
Familia* · Spain · 20th Century Over a century of
continual building has gone into this giant basilica
of intricate geometric and kaleidoscopic design by
Antoni Gaudí, intended to be a universal masterpiece of Christian symbolism.

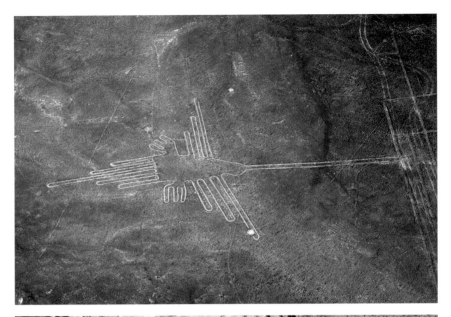

(opposite) Unknown *Swirling Nine-Pointed Star Formation* · England 1999 During a rare, total eclipse of the sun, visible in the English countryside, a plethora of crop circles appeared overnight. The nine-fold spinning star emerged just below the white horse hill figure at Cherhill. The crop circle phenomenon is concentrated in Wiltshire, with nearly four hundred found in the last thirty years.

Unknown · Nazca Lines in the Form of a Hummingbird · Peru · 200 BCE–600 CE The largest geoglyphs in the world, the Nazca lines can only be fully seen from an aerial view. Of the geometric design and shapes of plants and animals, the Hummingbird is the most iconic.

Unknown · *Anasazi of Pueblo Bonito* · United States 828–1126 A view of the ancient settlement displays the sophisticated architecture of the Anasazi civilization. This site is known as Pueblo Bonito and is located at Chaco Ruins Culture National Park, Chaco Canyon, New Mexico.

Unknown · *Buddhist Monk drawing a Sand Mandala*
France · 21st Century Steeped in philosophy and
rich in symbolism, the centuries-old art of creating
a sand mandala is a profound ritual. Shortly after
completion the mandala is destroyed as a symbol
of the impermanence of life.

Jean-Louis Nou · *Onam Festival in Kerala, India*
France · 1975 Onam, a Hindu harvest festival in
Kerala, is photographed as the fresh flower petal
mandala is completed. Created at the entrances of
homes, the mandalas ensure happiness and
prosperity.

THE ALCHEMY OF ARCHITECTURE

A Timeline

Mattia Bortoloni, Felice Biella, and Giuseppe Galli Bibiena *Sanctuary of Vicoforte* Italy · 1745–48 The assumption of Mary is painted on the cupola vault of the medieval sanctuary. Built around 1590, it was reconstructed after a passing-by hunter shot through a fresco of the Virgin Mary. Legend has it, she began to bleed. It has since become a pilgrimage site.

Since time immemorial our ancestors have activated the space around them in acts of worship and creative expression. The Blombos Cave in South Africa contains petroglyphs that date back to around 75,000 years ago, making them some of the earliest examples of rock art created by early humans. The petroglyphs in Blombos Cave consist of abstract symbols and patterns etched into pieces of ochre, a type of mineral pigment. These engravings are among the earliest forms of symbolic or artistic expression by Homo sapiens, demonstrating cognitive complexity and deep cultural significance.

17,000 BCE · Date of the first cave paintings made in Lascaux, France. These works are believed to have a spiritual or religious significance to the Upper Paleolithic peoples.

10,000 BCE · Uluru (Ayers Rock), Australia, a significant site to the local Aboriginal Anangu people, with evidence of human activity dating back to 10,000 BCE.

10,000–8,000 BCE · Göbekli Tepe in Turkey, the world's oldest known temple, is built, predating Stonehenge by 6,000 years.

3,200 BCE · Newgrange, a prehistoric monument located in County Meath, Ireland is built. A large circular mound with a stone passageway and chambers inside, Newgrange is best known for its intricate spiral carvings and its alignment with the winter solstice, where sunlight enters the passage and illuminates the inside of the chamber.

3,000–2,000 BCE · Stonehenge, a prehistoric monument with a circle of standing stones is erected. The site is possibly used for rituals or astronomical observations.

3,600–2,500 BCE · The Megalithic Temples of Malta are constructed. Among the oldest free-standing structures on Earth, some temples are believed to have been dedicated to a fertility deity.

2,580–2,560 BCE · The Great Pyramid of Giza, Egypt is built, the oldest of the Seven Wonders of the Ancient World and a monumental tomb for the Pharaoh Khufu.

2,055 BCE · Construction of the Great Temple of Amun at Karnak, Egypt begins. One of the largest religious buildings ever constructed, the temple is dedicated to the Theban triad of Amun, Mut, and Khonsu.

5th Century BCE · Varanasi is one of the oldest continuously inhabited cities in the world, located in the northern Indian state of Uttar Pradesh. The exact founding date of Varanasi is not definitively known, as the city has a history that spans thousands of years. It is a significant cultural, spiritual, and historical center in India, known for its ancient religious traditions, temples, ghats (riverfront steps), and the sacred Ganges River.

5th–4th Century BCE · Bodh Gaya, India, where Gautama Buddha attained enlightenment, is established, and becomes one of the most important pilgrimage sites for Buddhists.

PREHISTORIC ——— 3000 BCE ———

550 BCE · Temple of Artemis at Ephesus, Turkey, one of the Seven Wonders of the Ancient World, is built. The Temple was rebuilt multiple times due to destruction.

478 BCE · The Temple of Confucius, China is built, a temple and former residence of Confucius located in Qufu, Shandong Province. The temple was reconstructed in 2nd century.

438 BCE · The Parthenon is built in Athens, Greece, a temple dedicated to the goddess Athena, patroness of Athens.

300 BCE · Construction begins on La Danta, El Mirador. One of the largest pyramids by volume in the world, La Danta located in Guatemala and was a part of the Maya civilization.

100 BCE · Teotihuacan, Mexico is established, an ancient Mesoamerican city with pyramids and temples, central to the religious life of the region.

200 CE · Pyramid of the Sun, the largest pyramid in the ancient city of Teotihuacan, Mexico, and one of the largest in Mesoamerica is constructed. The second Pyramid of the Moon is constructed as well, standing at the end of Teotihuacan's Avenue of the Dead.

330 · Church of the Nativity, in Bethlehem, is built over what is traditionally considered the birthplace of Jesus Christ.

537 · The Hagia Sophia in Istanbul, Turkey, is completed. Originally constructed as a cathedral, it became one of the most important religious sites in the Christian and later Islamic worlds.

692 · First recorded construction of Ise Grand Shrine in Japan. The shrine is reconstructed every 20 years per Shinto traditions. Dedicated to the goddess Amaterasu, it is a major pilgrimage site for practitioners of Shinto.

850–1250 · Chaco Canyon, a major center of ancestral Pueblo culture was established. The site is known for its impressive architecture, including monumental stone buildings and a complex network of great houses, kivas (underground ceremonial chambers), and roads.

1163 · Construction begins on the Notre Dame Cathedral, also known simply as Notre Dame, a medieval Catholic cathedral located in the heart of Paris, France.

1194 · Construction begins of the Chartres Cathedral in France. A masterpiece of French Gothic architecture, known for its sacred relic, the Sancta Camisia.

7th Century · Mahabodhi Temple Complex, India is built, marking the location where Siddhartha Gautama, the Buddha, attained enlightenment.

7th Century · Glastonbury Abbey is founded becoming one of

the most important monasteries in England. It was built on the site of earlier religious structures and was expanded and renovated over the centuries. The abbey was known for its connections to King Arthur and the Holy Grail, and it was a popular pilgrimage destination during the Middle Ages.

8th Century · Parvati Temple in India is built, dedicated to the Hindu goddess Parvati, and located in Himachal Pradesh, India.

8th–12th Century · El Castillo (Temple of Kukulcán) is constructed. This step pyramid located at Chichen Itza in Mexico and is a testament to the sophistication of Maya civilization.

12th Century · Angkor Wat, Cambodia. Initially a Hindu temple dedicated to Vishnu, is built. It later became a Buddhist site and remains one of the largest religious monuments in the world.

13th–16th Century · The enormous sculptures of Easter Island, also known as Rapa Nui, a remote island in the Pacific Ocean, are first erected. The monumental statues, called moai were built by the indigenous Polynesian people of the island. The moai are large stone statues that represent ancestral figures.

15th Century · Machu Picchu is built by the Inca Empire, in the Andes Mountains. It served as a royal retreat and religious center,

500 BCE —— 1000 CE

dedicated to the Incan gods and the worship of nature. Today, it is a UNESCO World Heritage Site and a popular tourist destination.

15th Century · The Ryoan-ji Zen Garden in Kyoto is established, a renowned example of a dry rock garden that dates to the late 15th century and is known for its minimalist and meditative design.

16th Century · Temple of the Tooth is constructed in Sri Lanka to house the relic of the tooth of the Buddha and becomes a key site for Buddhist pilgrimage.

1604 · The Golden Temple, Amritsar, India is completed and is considered the holiest Gurdwara of Sikhism.

1626 · St. Peter's Basilica is built in Vatican City, the heart of the Catholic Church and one of the holiest sites in Christianity.

1709 · Basilica of Our Lady of Guadalupe, Mexico City, one of the most significant pilgrimage sites in Catholicism, especially among those of Mexican descent.

1858 · The Virgin Mary is said to have appeared to Bernadette Soubirous, a young peasant girl. The Grotto at Lourdes is subsequently founded on the site, a cave-like structure on the banks of the Gave de Pau River, in Lourdes, France.

1882 · Construction begins

(with anticipated completion in 2026) on Sagrada Familia, large Roman Catholic Basilica in Barcelona, designed by Catalan architect Antoni Gaudí.

1908 · First constructed in Ashgabat, Turkmenistan, Bahá'í Houses of Worship, are constructed at various locations. Of the nine continental temples, each has a unique design and together represent the Bahá'í principle of the oneness of humanity.

1934 · The Philosophical Research Library is built by Robert Judd in Los Angeles, California, USA. The space was founded by Manly P. Hall, a renowned author, lecturer, and philosopher. The library houses a vast collection of books, manuscripts, and esoteric materials on various philosophical, spiritual, and metaphysical topics.

1959 · New York's Guggenheim Museum opens to the public. Established by philanthropist Solomon R. Guggenheim and art advisor Hilla von Rebay, began in the late 1920s. In the 1940s, Guggenheim met architect Frank Lloyd Wright and commissioned him to design a new museum to house the growing collection. Construction of the now iconic spiral-shaped building began in 1956.

1964 · Construction begins on Sea Ranch, planned community located along the rugged coastline of northern California, USA.

It was designed as a residential development in the mid-1960s by a team of architects, including Lawrence Halprin, Joseph Esherick, and Charles Moore.

1965 · Drop City is founded, an experimental community and art project in southern Colorado, USA. It was established by a group of artists and countercultural individuals seeking to create a communal living environment that embraced artistic expression, environmental sustainability, and alternative lifestyles.

1968 · *The Whole Earth Catalogue*, a counterculture publication and catalog created by Stewart Brand, was first published. The Catalogue had a significant impact on the environmental movement, the back-to-the-land movement, and the development of the internet and personal computing.

1970 · The Pilton Pop, Folk & Blues Festival is founded and renamed the Glastonbury Festival in 1971. The Glastonbury Festival has since grown into one of the world's most iconic and largest music festivals. Glastonbury is known for its unique blend of music, arts, culture, and community spirit, as well as its commitment to sustainability and charitable causes.

1970 · Building begins on Arcosanti, the experimental town and arcology project designed by architect Paolo Soleri.

1900

Construction on Arcosanti is still ongoing, and the site serves as a live-in workshop for the development and realization of Soleri's architectural and ecological concepts.

1970 · Spiral Jetty is built by artist Robert Smithson, considered a seminal work of land art that explores the relationship between nature, art, and the environment. The sculpture is approximately 1,500 feet long and 15 feet wide, creating a distinctive and striking form that interacts with the changing water levels of the Great Salt Lake.

1971 · Christiania is established. Also known as Freetown Christiania, it is a self-proclaimed autonomous neighborhood and anarchist community located in the Christianshavn district of Copenhagen, Denmark.

1973 · The Sun Tunnels began to be constructed, with completion in 1976. The installation was designed by American artist Nancy Holt, known for her pioneering work in land art and her exploration of light, space, and time in her artistic practice.

1978 · Construction begins on the Tarot Garden, also known as Giardino dei Tarocchi, a sculpture park located in Tuscany, Italy. It was created by the French artist Niki de Saint Phalle and opened to the public in 1998. The Tarot Garden features monumental sculptures inspired by the tarot

Lauren Halsey · The eastside of south central los angeles hieroglyph prototype architecture (I) United States · 2022
The Met rooftop garden was commissioned to Halsey, who created a self-standing and site-specific installation. Combining elements of Afrofuturism, Egyptian symbolism, and the concerns faced by people of color, queer, the working class, and her own South Central Los Angeles community, she fluidly merges ancient and current history.

cards, with each sculpture representing a different card from the tarot arcana.

1979 · Artist James Turrell acquires the Roden Crater, a dormant volcanic crater located in the Painted Desert region of northern Arizona, USA, and begins his iconic large-scale land art project.

1982 · The artist Agnes Denes' created Wheatfield, her iconic land art project, planting a two-acre wheat field in a landfill located in lower Manhattan, near the site of where the former World Trade Center towers stood.

1986 · Bahá'í House of Worship (Lotus Temple) is completed. A Bahá'í House of Worship in New Delhi, India, the temple is notable for its flowerlike shape.

1986 · Larry Harvey and Jerry James build and burn an 8-foot-tall wooden effigy on a San Francisco beach. Over the years, the event became known as Burning Man, an annual gathering now held in the Black Rock Desert of Nevada, USA. Burning Man is characterized by its principles of radical self-expression, communal participation, decommodification, and environmental stewardship.

1995 · "Spiral of Time" is created by Richard Long. A large-scale installation consisting of a spiral pathway created with stones and other natural materials by the British Land artist.

2003 · The Chapel of Sacred Mirrors, often referred to as CoSM, is founded. A sanctuary and contemporary temple located in Wappingers Falls, New York, USA, it was created by visionary artists Alex Grey and Allyson Grey. The chapel serves as a spiritual and artistic hub, dedicated to the celebration of creativity, consciousness expansion, and visionary art.

2008 · Meow Wolf, an arts and entertainment collective based in Santa Fe, New Mexico, is founded by a group of artists, writers, and musicians. The group is known for its immersive, interactive art experiences, which often involve multiple mediums and storytelling elements. The first permanent installation created by Meow Wolf, called the House of Eternal Return, opened in March 2016 in Santa Fe.

2000s–Present · Artists and seekers across the globe continue to express their creativity and spirituality through various forms of architecture, gardens, sculptures, installations, and immersive works as well as in performance, pilgrimage, dance, prayer, and communal gatherings.

1970 ———— 1980 ———— 2000

Keep Moving Forward
ho Ye Is.
ain't who you
o you think
Is.
We WE out THERE
IN Here
Restoring Hope
REFLECTION
BUILD AUTON
SOLIDAR
LOOK
WHAT
YOU CREATED
a lil this...a lil that
SLAUSON
MY HOPE
Positive Energy

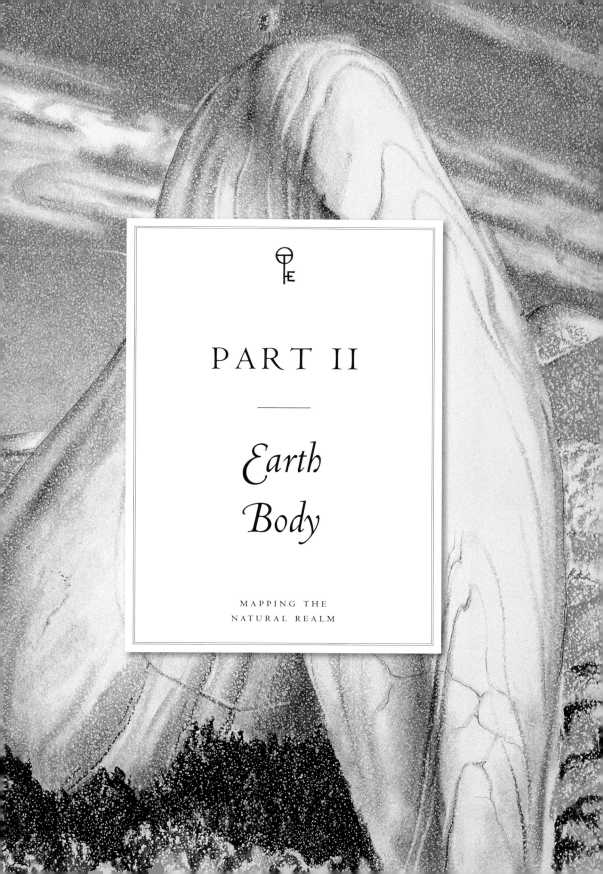

PART II

—

Earth
Body

MAPPING THE
NATURAL REALM

HOLY MOTHER

Worshiping at Nature's Altar

The earth is a living, conscious being. In company with cultures of many different times and places, we name these things as sacred: air, fire, water, and earth. Whether we see them as the breath, energy, blood, and body of the Mother, or as the blessed gifts of a Creator, or as symbols of the interconnected systems that sustain life, we know that nothing can live without them.

— STARHAWK, Author, Activist, and Eco-Feminist, from *The Fifth Sacred Thing*, 1993

Lita Albuquerque
NAJMA (She Placed One Thousand Suns Over the Transparent Overlays of Space) · **United States 2020** Set in Desert X AlUla of Saudi Arabia and other deserts around the world, Albuquerque installs the story art of Elyseria, an ultramarine blue pigmented female astronaut who comes to earth in 6000 BCE. Her mission is to teach about the stars, but she forgets her purpose before eventually reconnecting with the star keepers.

Our home planet, nurturing us, sustaining all life as we know it, is perhaps the most sacred site of all. Looking back to the rites of our prehistoric ancestors, to their rituals dedicated to the divinity of soil, of the plants and trees, of oceans and skies, we have long associated the earth as an expression of the divine. The first goddess we bowed to in worship was the Earth herself, the divine mother, embodied in the wind-blown branches, in the rise of stone and mountain, in the flow of rapids and in the moon—held tides. Spiritual sites were all around us—our ancestors embracing various forms of animism, the belief that all things, including the Earth, is alive and possesses spirit. Animistic cultures often held ceremonies to honor this deep connection to nature, making offerings and engaging in communal rituals. Many simply observed and revered the natural world, recognizing it as a manifestation of the divine.

Throughout human history, we have worshipped the Earth and nature, often attributing sacred qualities to various natural entities such as trees, mountains, rivers, and soil. Animism can be found in most indigenous cultures around the world. These polytheistic, nature-based spiritual traditions long predated monotheism and even today, modern pagan movements such as Wicca, place a strong emphasis on the sacredness of the Earth and its cycles. Earth-based Spirituality is another modern non-institutionalized spiritual approach that views Earth as a mother and encourages fostering a harmonious relationship with the natural world.

Gaia Philosophy, which emerged in the late 20th century, first proposed by scientist James Lovelock, is a scientific and spiritual perspective that views Earth as a single self-regulating, complex system, the Gaia, which encompasses all living beings. The word "Gaia" originates from ancient Greek

(previous pages) Stanislav Szukalski · *Erotic Landscape* · Poland · 1954 The radical convictions of Szukalski imbued his art with captivating morphs of human and animal bodies with mythological creatures, ancient art, and the natural world.

mythology. Thought to be the personification of the Earth, she was one of the primordial deities who emerged at the creation of the universe. According to Hesiod's *Theogony*, Gaia was the mother of everything, the foundation of all the gods and of the world itself. She emerged from Chaos and gave birth to Uranus (the Sky), Pontus (the Sea), and the Titans, among other beings. In some myths, Gaia is considered the original deity from whom all others descend.

Shamanism is another long-held tradition directly related to the power of the elements and nature. Practiced by indigenous tribes globally, shamanism often involves a practitioner reaching altered states of consciousness into order to interact with a spirit world. The shaman then channels these transcendental energies for the community's

benefit, often engaging directly with the forces of nature and plant medicines. Religions such as Hinduism also reflect a profound reverence for the Earth. Certain rivers, such as the Ganges and other natural sites, are considered holy in Hinduism, true expressions of the divine. The core teachings of Buddhism also convey a respect for all life and an understanding of our interdependence with the natural world. In Japanese Shinto practices, ceremonies often involve the worship of spirits known as "kami," which are associated with elements found in nature. In North America, indigenous cultures have long held a profound respect for the Earth, often seeing themselves as stewards of the land, with spiritual practices that honor the interconnectedness of all life. In Taoism, a philosophy and religion originating in ancient China, there

Unknown · *Torre des Savinar and Es Vedra island at Dawn* · Spain · 1750s Photographed in the first morning light, the mysteriously built tower hovers above the sea with Es Vedra island in sight, the third most energetic place on earth. Many posit it to be a lost piece of Atlantis.

Keisai Eisen · *Kegon Waterfall* · Japan · 19th Century Within the Nikko National Park flows one of Japan's most scenic attractions, the breathtaking Kegon Falls, a three hundred and fifteen-foot cascading waterfall. Revered as a pilgrimage site, the falls takes its name from the Buddhist text.

is an emphasis on living in harmony with the Tao, which is often understood as the fundamental nature of the world.

Gods and goddesses representing nature have also been integral to the mythologies and religious traditions across various cultures. For the Greeks, Demeter was called the goddess of the Earth, of harvest and fertility. In Norse myth, Freyr was the god of sunlight and rain, presiding over the life-giving forces of nature. Freya was goddess of love and often associated with plant life and the earth. In Hinduism, Prithvi is known as the Mother goddess, representing fertility and nature. For the ancient Celts, Danu was considered the ancestral goddess of the earth, while Cernunnos was worshipped as

the horned god of the animals, of forests, and fertility. And among the diverse indigenous tribes across the Americas, there are many nature deities, such as the Hopi Corn Mother Kachina and the Cherokee spirit of the Earth. In Aztec myth, Tlaloc is considered the god of rain, water, and fertility and Xochiquetzal is thought to be the goddess of flowers and love. For the ancient Incans, Pachamama was the great goddess of the earth and was revered as the mother of all. Each of these deities represent the myriad of ways we create deeper connections between the divine and the natural world, the sacred link between soil and skies, life-giving plants and waters, and the great miracle of human form and consciousness.

David Reed · *Uluru/Ayers Rock at Sunset* · England Date Unknown Spiritually significant to the aboriginal people in Australia, Uluru is thought to be the navel at the center of the Earth, implicit in their creation story or "Dreamtime."

Bret Agre · *The Great Serpent Mound* · United States · 2007 Built by indigenous peoples of North America around 1070, The Great Serpent in Ohio is one of the biggest effigy mounds in the world.

Federico Faruffini · *The Sacrifice of a Virgin to the Nile*
Italy · 1865 Painted in romanticism style, Faruffini
gives vision to the myth that ancient Egyptians sacri-
ficed a virgin to the Nile to instigate the Nile flood.
According to the mythology, the flood was the tears
of Isis, crying over the loss of her beloved Osiris.

(following, left) Caspar David Friedrich · *Chalk Cliffs at Rügen* · Germany · 1818 Friedrich's highly allegorical and mystical painting was done after he and his wife visited the chalk cliffs in Rügen. Every detail imparts meaning about life—both eternal and impermanent.

(following, right) Tomás Sánchez · *Contempladores de cascadas* · France · 1992 As a lifelong meditator, Sanchez creates from visions and higher states of consciousness.

I've always been super sensitive to the land around me. Growing up in North Africa and Tunisia and Carthage, I was surrounded by history. All the Roman ruins were below me, and I had a very deep sense of what was in the earth. Then when I came to America, I lived in an artist colony, 132 acres of land overlooking the ocean, and that's when I did my first ephemeral piece, which was a blue line going all the way out to the horizon. Perceptually it looked like a cross. The materials I've always worked with, from the start of my career, are natural and the very first pieces I made were created from rocks and pigment. I covered the rocks in colored pigment to convey the idea that light is embedded in matter. When I put pigment on rocks, it's the idea of revealing the light that's within the stone. I began by wanting to not have anything in my work that was manmade, so I started with using only rocks and ground-up rocks and mineral pigments. Then, from there, I went to copper for its reflectivity and then to gold for its illumination and then on and on to other things, like performance and film. I was always interested in using sacred geometry and the body to connect all these alignment points, to those spaces on the horizon and to the stars themselves. The very first piece I made was tracing the horizon line and wanting to connect to that horizon in some way. For me, that line held a tremendous amount of longing. More than anything, my work is about connecting the body to the horizon and from there, about the need to align the body to the stars. To me, each individual star is a different kind of opening, a different kind of reception that you get from it. In that way sacred sites, many of which are aligned astronomically to the movements of the cosmos, allow you to feel that longing for connection in a profound way.

— LITA ALBUQUERQUE, Scholar & Meditation Teacher, 2024

Unknown · *Giant Redwood Trees in Stout Memorial Grove California* · United States · Date Unknown
Standing as forest guardians at over three hundred and forty feet, some believe the redwoods morphed from people and animals, the crimson color reminding us that we are all of the same blood.

EARTH

I enter as a sacred place, a Sanctum sanctorum. There is the strength, in the marrow, of Nature.

— HENRY DAVID THOREAU, Author, Philosopher, and Seeker, from *Walking (The Wild)*, 1851

(following, left)
Joseph Stella · *Tree of My Life* · **United States** · 1919 The Italian American artist Joseph Stella was a leader in the Futurist Painting Movement, depicting modernized interpretations of sacred and spiritual themes, often set within industrialized landscapes and architecture.

Rich with sustaining life, the plants and trees that nurture and protect us, the earth, in nearly all indigenous spiritual traditions, is thought to be the realm of an ancient and fertile mother goddess, with the ground itself inherently an elemental aspect of all worship and ritual. In many belief systems of this kind, the earth is said to represent themes of abundance and fertility, with ceremonies often centered on connecting and communing with the natural world. Rites were celebrated with the seasons, as dictated by the reaping, and sowing of the land, of planting and harvest.

In Greek mythology, earth was said to be the embodiment of the ancestral feminine, a being named Gaia, considered the first primordial deity. In ancient Egyptian culture—its attributes were masculine, as embodied by Geb, the God of Earth and Land. In these myths, earth deities are often aligned with chthonic gods and goddess, the Underworld a realm existing as part of (and inherent to) their domain. The concepts of death and rebirth, of the cold seed placed under soil to gestate and sprout, are all integrated into these traditions through various acts of worship. Milk or blood is spilled in ritual and offered to the soil. Ceremonial dances are performed on sacred lands. In certain modern pagan practices such as Wicca, Earth as an element is associated with the direction of the north and the season of winter—a moment of isolation and inward growth, of grounding and gestation—and therefore ceremonial offerings are often buried deeply under dirt or placed on outdoor altars built upon sanctified grounds.

Around the world there are also certain specific locations which are considered sacrosanct within numerous cultures and religions—often these places are associated with key moments in the mythologies of deities or in the lives (and deaths) of spiritual leaders. Bodh Gaya, India for instance, is considered the most sacred site in Buddhism, as it is believed to be the place where Gautama Buddha first attained enlightenment. Another location in India, Varanasi, is considered by Hindus to be a holy space as it is believed to be the exact spot where Shiva and Parvati stood when time first began. In North America, an area known the Black Hills of South Dakota is considered sacred by many indigenous tribes, including the Lakota, Cheyenne, and Arapaho—the lands in this area thought to be the very center of the spiritual universe.

Joos de Momper the Younger · *Anthropomorphic Landscape* · **Belgium** · ca. 1600 Although Momper was more known for his realism landscape paintings of rock and slope formations, he stylized more than his contemporaries, bringing fantasy elements to a usually naturalistic style.

(opposite, top) Georgia O'Keeffe · *Pelvis with Distance* · United States · 1943 A rare surrealist vision of a distorted perspective of an animal hip girdle, from the artist known for her provocative depictions of flowers, is one of a series of pelvis paintings.

(opposite, bottom) Paul Cézanne · *Montagne Sainte-Victoire with Large Pine* · France · ca. 1887 Cézanne's vantage point from his home in Aix-en-Provence, of the iconic limestone mountain range which was the subject of many of his paintings.

STONE

There is life in a stone. Any stone that sits in a field or lies on a beach takes on the memory of that place. You can feel that stones have witnessed so many things.

— ANDY GOLDSWORTHY, Sculptor, Photographer, and Environmental Artist, 2003

The flicker of firelight illuminating the carved slope of boulder, the rise of monolithic rock emerging from verdant green grass, from giant cliffs to simple ceremonial offerings made upon an altar of ancient quartz—stone, enduring, eternal—is an integral element in sacred sites and rituals around the globe. There are the hand-hewn rock temples of the ancients, the circle at Stonehenge, the looming heads of Easter Island, the exquisite vine-covered shrines of Cambodia.

Distinctive natural rock formations have also long been venerated across cultures—towering stone sanctuaries carved by rain and wind are often worshipped as domains of the gods themselves—sites where ceremony and offerings have been made since millennia. There is the steep rise of Dogon Cliffs in Mali, Africa for instance, considered sacred by the Dogon people, with rocks here intricately decorated with imagery representing the Dogon's spiritual and cosmological beliefs. In Q'enqo, Peru near the city of Cusco, the area's elaborately carved stone formations are thought to have been an important ceremonial site for the Incas—a place of worship and ritual.

The monumental table-like rise of the Ayers Rock (also known as Uluru) in Australia, continues to hold a deep spiritual significance for the area's indigenous Anangu people. In North America, Bear's Lodge Wyoming, sometimes called Devil's Tower, is a red rock formation long sacred to numerous tribes. For centuries this place, (like Uluru, an otherworldly formation of stone emerging abruptly from a relatively flat and remote landscape) has been a central meeting place for prayer and ceremony.

Another site sacred to both indigenous peoples and to modern seekers as well, is Sedona, Arizona in the vastness of the American Southwest. Thought to be located upon various highly energetic leylines and vortexes, the area's distinctive rock formations, rising, burnt orange against deep azure sky, also add to the mystical allure of this place, which has been a home to various spiritual and New Age communities for the last century.

Homer Sykes · *Stonehenge Free Festival at the summer solstice* · **Canada/England** · 1979 During the seventies and early eighties, the prehistoric locale held a music fest at solstice which grew to nearly thirty thousand visitors and drew names like Hawkwind, The Raincoats, Dexy's Midnight Runners, and Jimmy Page.

Frances Broomfield · *Avebury* · England · 1983
Southwest England's site of three prehistoric, neolithic period stone circles, is believed to be built on
ley lines by druids. It remains an important pagan
ceremonial site, thought to have an astrological
connection to Stonehenge.

Martin Puddy · *The golden rock of Kayaiktiyo at sunrise*
Myanmar · Date Unknown Appearing to magically
perch on the side of a boulder, Kyaikteyo rock is
said to be held in place by a hair from the Buddha,
enshrined there and topped with a pagoda to
honor him.

WATER

Water is the driving force of all nature.

— LEONARDO DA VINCI, Artist, Inventor, and Seeker, 1501

Symbolic in many pagan traditions as representing the sacred feminine—water is life itself, the sustaining force that nurtures us—both in the womb and beyond. Water has long been considered a sacred element in cultures around the globe. One of the most significant bodies of water is the Ganges River in India, considered a holy river by Hindus and believed to purify one's soul if one bathes in its waters. The river is also believed to be a goddess, Ganga, who descended to earth to cleanse the sins of the people. Every year, millions of pilgrims travel to the Ganges to take a dip in its waters during the Kumbh Mela, a Hindu festival.

Another important sacred water site is the Zamzam well in Mecca, Saudi Arabia. It is one of the holiest sites in Islam and is believed to have been discovered by the biblical figure Hagar and her son Ishmael. The well's water is considered to have healing properties and is also used in religious rituals, including the Hajj pilgrimage. Lake Titicaca, located on the border of Peru and Bolivia, is also considered a sacred body of water. It is believed to be the birthplace of the Inca civilization, and the lake's islands are home to many ancient temples and ruins. The peoples who live around the lake still practice traditional customs and

religious rituals, including offerings to the spirits of the lake.

The Jordan River, located in the Middle East, is another important sacred water space, believed to be the site where Jesus Christ was baptized by John the Baptist. Lake Baikal in Russia is the world's deepest lake and is a sacred site for the Buryat people, a Mongolian ethnic group. They consider the lake to be a living organism and believe that it possesses a spirit. For them, the lake is a source of all life and a symbol of the universe's unity. Finally, the Nile River in Egypt has been considered a sacred river since antiquity. The ancient Egyptians considered the river to be the embodiment of the god Hapi, who brought them fertility and prosperity. The river's annual flooding was a significant event in the religious calendar, and many temples were constructed along its banks.

Sacred waters around the globe continue to hold significant cultural and religious importance, each a reflection of a diverse range of beliefs and traditions. To visit these waters in veneration and worship is considered by many to be a path to redemption and to both physical and spiritual healing.

(previous pages) Jeaneen Lund · *Embryo* · United States · 2012 Photographed in the magickal realm of the Icelandic landscape, the elements of water, earth, and air combine in this surrealistic image from the California-based photographer and director.

John William Waterhouse · *The Danaïdes* · England 1906 The Danaïdes were bound to punishment for eternity for killing their husband by perpetually carrying jugs of water to fill a basin. Their release would come only when the basin became full.

Todd Weaver · *David Viz Malibu Nose Ride* United States · 2021 Weaver has an eye for waves and an affinity for surfing them. He contrasts his subject matter through manipulation of color, shade, double exposures, and blurring, imbuing his work with a sense of wonder.

Marie-Dominique Siciliano · *The gorges of El Kantara in southern Algeria* · Italy · 19th Century An oasis considered to be the gateway to the deserts of Algiers, the gorges of El Kantara is one of the most important caravan stations.

Joseph Stella · *Apotheosis of the Rose* · United States 1926 A key figure in the Futurist Movement, Stella was known for his expressive visions of spaces and landmarks, from his images of industrialized America to his explorations of imaginary dreamscapes.

Maria Filopoulou
Underwater Swimmer
Greece · 2002 Union
with nature is easily
found in water envi-
ronments, bringing
happiness and relax-
ation without effort.
Filopoulou imparts this
relationship to water
in her paintings that
express her experiences
in aquatic Edens.

Boris Kustodiev
Bathing Russia · 1912
Kustodiev captures
the beauty of the free
human spirit in nature's
embrace while his
own health left him
paraplegic and unable
to leave his room. His
ability to maintain and
express his creative gift
was remarkable and
seemingly vicarious.

(opposite) Julia
Morgan · *Hearst Castle
roman pool* · United
States · 1927–34
Statues of Roman Gods
and Goddesses and
marble and alabaster
lamps flank the exqui-
site mosaic pool at the
famed estate featuring
one hundred sixty-five
rooms. Built to show-
case the art collection
of William Randolph
Hearst, upon his death
he willed the castle to
the state of California.

SKY

The sky is the daily bread of the eyes.

— RALPH WALDO EMERSON, Writer, Philosopher, and Seeker, 1836

The heavens high above speak to us in a complex language, from the brilliant spread of stars in the blackness of night, to the tempestuous, emotive array of weather patterns—storm and sun giving the sky its eloquence and power. Since the very dawn of humanity, the celestial realm has been revered, with cultures around the world developing intricate belief systems linked to the movement and influence of the heavens.

The ancient Egyptians were one of the first civilizations to develop a complex mythology around the sky, believing it to be a manifestation of the god Horus, one of their most important deities, often depicted as a falcon or a man with a falcon head. In Egyptian tradition, the deceased were believed to be reborn into the sky, where they would live alongside the gods. The Greeks also revered the sky, considering it to be the domain of Zeus. According to Greek mythology, Zeus controlled the weather and was responsible for lightning bolts, thunder, and other natural phenomena. This worship of the sky was also reflected in their architecture, with their temples often featuring skylights to symbolize the divine presence of the heavens.

In ancient China, the sky was worshipped as a powerful force through the traditional philosophy of Taoism. Taoism considers the sky to be one of the three principal gods of the universe, along with the earth and water. The Inca civilization of South America also worshipped the sky, considering it to be the domain of the god Inti, who represented the sun. Inca culture emphasized the importance of Inti in all aspects of life, with the sun being a symbol of power and prosperity. In North America, the Navajo people also worship the sky through their traditional religion of Diné. The Diné believe the sky to be manifestation of the Diyin Dine'é, the god responsible for creating and sustaining all life on earth. Navajo culture emphasizes the interconnectedness of all things in nature, with the sky being considered an essential link in the complex web of relationships between humans, animals, plants, and the planet.

The sky continues to shape our lives and our world in the most profound of ways, its influence affecting the air we breathe, the movement of the tides, the rains and sun that nurture the rich soil below. Through our worship of the heavens, through myths, symbology, and ritual, we honor our integral connection to the mystery of the universe itself.

Pál Szinyei Merse · *The Lark* · Hungary · 1882
Impressionist nude focusing on the nature of human and earth companionship as the subject gazes at the skylark flying above. Sky and earth and body intimately connect in this mythic dreamscape by the Hungarian artist.

Winslow Homer *Moonlight* · United States · 1874 Known for his love for the sea, bodies of water featured repeatedly in his watercolor works. He masterfully expressed intensity, beauty, and drama in his highly regarded seascapes reflecting open skies.

Vincent Van Gogh *Wheat Fields with Cypresses* · Netherlands 1889 The psychedelic skies in Van Gogh's paintings swell with color and effect. Much inquiry has gone into the intention underlying his atmospheric and dimensional heavens. Towering into those heavens are cypresses amid wheat which were in view from his asylum room in St. Remy.

(opposite) Étienne Léopold Trouvelot · *Part of the Milky Way* · France · 1881–82 Craters on the Moon and Mars are named after Trouvelot, who, after witnessing the northern lights, left a career as an entomologist to become an astronomer and artist. He illustrated his astronomical observations and made over 7,000 of them. Although meant to be scientific, they are mesmerizing works.

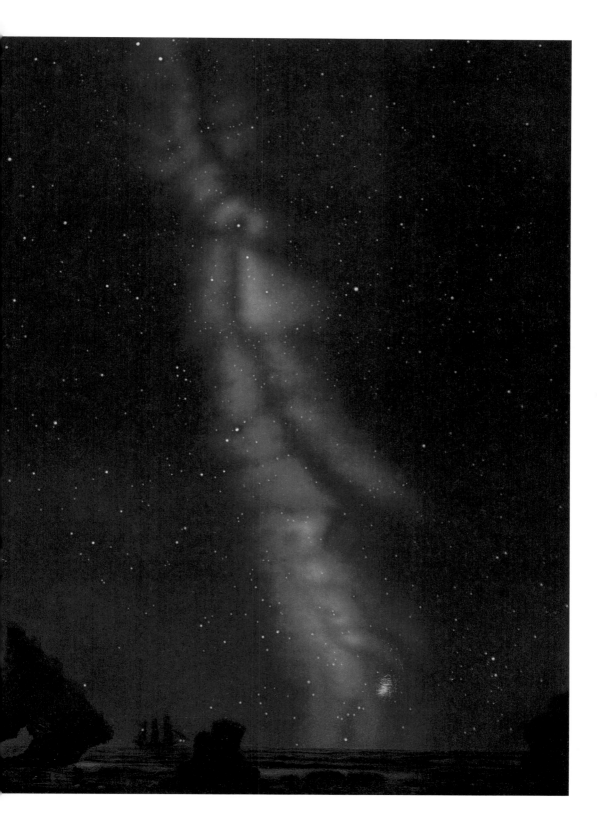

MOUNTAINS

*Climb the mountains and get their good tidings. Nature's peace will flow into you as sunshine
flows into trees. The winds will blow their own freshness into you, and the storms their energy,
while cares will drop away from you like the leaves of Autumn.*

— JOHN MUIR, Writer, Environmentalist, from The Mountains of California, 1882

In mythologies around the globe, the mountain is often thought to be the realm of gods. In ancient Greek culture, Mount Olympus was considered to be the home where the most important deities resided and in many other cultures, the towering mountaintop peaks are often revered as symbols of strength, endurance, and spiritual power. High in the Swiss Alps, The Matterhorn was long considered a sacred mountain by Pre-Christian pagans, believed to be the home of the god of thunder, and when its peaks were shrouded in clouds it was believed to be the breath of the god.

The rise of rock and cliff, the meeting of land and sky, sacred mountains appear in the mythical storytelling and in the scriptures and teachings of nearly all major religions. Mount Kailash in Tibet, for instance, is considered the most sacred mountain in the world by four different religions: Hinduism, Buddhism, Jainism, and Bon. It is believed to be the home of the god Shiva and is considered the source of spiritual power and enlightenment. Pilgrims from around the world travel to Mount Kailash to perform the Kora, a ritual circumambulation of the mountain. In Egypt, Mount Sinai is also regarded as sacred in numerous religions, particularly in Judaism and Christianity, as it

is believed to be the mountain where Moses received the Ten Commandments.

Mount Fuji in Japan is also considered a sacred mountain associated with the Shinto goddess Sengen-Sama, who is believed to inhabit the mountain's peak. Mount Fuji is also revered by Buddhists and has been the site of many spiritual pilgrimages throughout history. In Hawaii, Mauna Kea is sacred to the Native Hawaiians, considered the realm of deities and revered for its spiritual significance. In North America, Mount Shasta in Northern California is thought to be a powerful energetic center, the mountain a sacred site for many indigenous peoples in the region, including the Shasta, Karuk, and Modoc, who associate the mountain with spiritual power, symbolic of both strength and transformation.

Around the world, the mountain is considered sacrosanct, across countless mythologies and religions, a place seen as a bridge between the earthly and the spiritual realm. In most global cultures these rugged peaks offer a connection to a higher power, to deities and divine beings. Our ancestors believed that by ascending the long path upward toward the mountain top, one might ultimately journey into the netherworlds beyond.

Caspar David Friedrich · *Wanderer Above the Sea of Fog* · Germany · 1818 A man stands amongst a dense sea of fog atop rocky peaks seemingly contemplating the unknown. Friedrich often included a small human element amid his allegorical panoramas, to depict nature's awe-inspiring power over humanity's fragile understanding of such.

Penny Slinger
Journeys End
England/United States
1976–77 Mountain
summits abound
in a series of Tantric
collages from the book
Mountain Ecstasy, in
an attempt to redefine
pornography as sacred
and impersonal, a
human right and path-
way to spiritual heights.

Lawren S. Harris
Mount Robson · Canada
ca. 1929 The highest
peak in the Canadian
Rockies in modernist
style from Theosophist
and 'Group of Seven'
artist Harris, is among
his many depictions
of his simple and
stark mountainous
landscapes.

(opposite)
Edward S. Curtis
*Bare Chested Tewa Man
Standing on a Cliff*
United States · 1927
A Tewa man offers
cornmeal in a daily
mountain ritual. Curtis
photographed many
native people practicing
ceremony, ritual, and
spiritual alliance with
nature to record their
cultural significance
which was disregarded
and erased through
Anglo ignorance.

FORESTS & GROVES

It seemed absolutely obvious that the church of the Earth was the greatest church of all; that the temple of the forest was the supreme temple.

— JOHN P. MILTON, Author & Meditation Teacher, from *Sky Above, Earth Below,* 1999

Forests have long been revered throughout the world as sacred spaces—trees themselves believed to possess spiritual power in numerous pagan and indigenous traditions across the globe. The ancient Celts considered the oak sacred, the tree thought to be a symbol of strength, endurance, and wisdom. In ancient Europe, the evergreen tree was associated with immortality and rebirth, its eventual association with Christmas believed to have been adopted and integrated into the Christian holiday from its early roots in Northern European pagan traditions.

The concept of the forest itself as sacred space, animated by spirit and emanating an energy entirely its own, can be found in many global cultures. In the Amazon, for instance, the world's largest tropical rainforest is considered sacred by many indigenous communities in South America. Their complex mythologies claim the forest to be a potent source of life and sustenance. The Hoh Rainforest, located in North America, is considered sacred by the indigenous Quileute Tribe. As their ancestral home, the Quileute believe the Hoh not only to have the ability to heal the wounded and sick, but to also be the home of the spirits of their ancestors. In Japan, the cedar forests

of the Kumano region have been considered sacred since ancient times. Here it is believed that deities reside in the trees, and visitors to the forest are encouraged to pray for good luck and blessings. The forest is also home to the Kumano Kodo pilgrimage route, considered one of the most sacred pilgrimage routes in all of Japan.

In Uganda, Africa, the Bwindi Impenetrable Forest is considered sacred by the Batwa people. The Batwa rely on the forest for their food, medicine, and cultural practices, and have been stewards of the land for centuries. The Daintree Rainforest in Australia is considered sacred by the Kuku Yalanji Aboriginal people who have lived there for over 50,000 years. In their stories and mythologies, the forest itself is believed to be their ancestor and every living being in the forest possesses a spirit.

Trees and forests, with their magical transformation of carbon dioxide to oxygen, their labyrinthian root systems and towering spreads of branches—not only help to sustain and nurture all life on earth, but also offer sources of spiritual inspiration—objects of worship and veneration for numerous cultures around the globe.

Gustaf Wilhelm Palm · *Cypresses Study* · **Sweden 1843** The mournful tree of lore, sacred to Diana and Apollo, is a common symbol in art, as with Palm's realistic landscape dedicated to the tree of both life and death.

Claude Monet · *Olive
Trees in The Moreno
Garden* · France · 1884
With written permission
from the Moreno's,
Monet was allowed to
visit the famed gardens
which inspired many
of his olive tree paint-
ings. As the garden
property was eventually
subdivided, a small
public-view portion was
named Monet Gardens.

Unknown · *Radha and
Krishna Embracing in a
Grove of Flowering Trees*
India · ca. 1780 Often
depicted in a flowering
grove symbolizing
their union, Radha
and Krishna expressed
their love among the
sweet-smelling shade
of Kadamba trees. They
represent divine union
between the individual
and universal self.

(opposite) Unknown
Mystical Landscape
Iran · 1398
The Timurid empire of
Iran and Central Asia
flourished in art and
architecture as part of
a powerfully creative
national identity.
The Timurid miniature
painting is from a
collection of Persian
poetry. The painters
were skilled masters
and highly regarded.

Charles E. Burchfield
Childhood's Garden
United States · 1917
Fantasy, memory, and
mysticism permeate the
nature scene of both
foreboding darkness
and rays from heaven.
Speaking to his process,
Burchfield said, "To be
inside of a building shut
in from the outdoors,
sometimes only makes
the outdoors more vivid."

(opposite, top) Eyvind Earle · *Mist in the Dark
Woods* · United States · 1992 Disney artist Earle
was able to bring an inspired synthesis of highly
stylized artistry to his forests as he was constantly
captivated by their grandeur and power.

(opposite, bottom) C. W. Röhrig · *Oak Forest*
Germany · 1984 The destruction of the forests
inspired Röhrig's 'Forest Series,' a collection of central European woodland scenes. Much of his art
centered around consciousness of the environment
and endangered species.

CAVES & GROTTOES

The very cave you are afraid to enter, turns out to be the source of what you are looking for. . .
I enter as a sacred place, a Sanctum sanctorum. There is the strength, in the marrow, of Nature.

— JOSEPH CAMPBELL, Author, Mythologist, and Seeker, from *Reflections on the Art of Living*, 1851

Perhaps the first spiritual spaces, providing shelter and protection to our ancestors, caves and grottos have long been considered sacred across cultures. In some mythologies, caves are believed to be a conduit between the physical and spiritual, a mystical pathway between two worlds. In nearly every belief system around the globe, the cave and grotto dark, mysterious, and womblike, retain their importance, even today, as destinations for both ritual and pilgrimage.

In Israel, the Holy Cross Grotto, located inside the Church of the Holy Sepulchre in Jerusalem, remains a popular site of Christian pilgrimage, believed to be the place where Jesus was crucified, buried, and resurrected. The Grotto of the Nativity, in Bethlehem, located in a cave beneath the Church of the Nativity, is also a sacred site, considered by Christians to be the birthplace of Jesus. And on the island of Patmos in Greece, a site known as the Grotto of the Apocalypse, is thought to be where Saint John the Evangelist received the visions that inspired the Book of Revelation.

Across the globe, in Malaysia, the ancient Batu Caves still serve as a sacred Hindu shrine, dedicated to the Hindu god of war. In India, the Ajanta Caves are considered one of the most important Buddhist sites in the world. A vast complex consisting of numerous carved rock caves, the site is thought to date back to the 2nd century BCE Long a place of spiritual pilgrimage, the walls of Ajanta are covered in elaborate art, decorated with intricate paintings and murals. In New Zealand, the Waitomo Caves are considered sacred by the Māori people. The caves are home to thousands of glowworms, which emit a soft blue light believed by the Māori to be the eyes of the god of the underworld.

At the Lourdes Grotto in France, Catholic pilgrims flock to Sanctuary of Our Lady of Lourdes, the site where the Virgin Mary is believed to have appeared to Saint Bernadette in 1858. In Spain, the prehistoric cave known as Altamira, contains some of the world's oldest cave paintings, dating as far back as the Paleolithic period, nearly 36,000 years ago. Here, ancient artworks mark the rugged rock walls, smooth-lined sketches of animals and delicately-drawn charcoal tracings of human hands—proof perhaps, that the desire to create, to communicate, to leave our mark on the world, was as resonate then—as now.

Pablo Picasso · *Minotaur and Mare before a Cave* Spain · 1936 One of the works from the commissioned "Vollard Suite" features the artist's beloved minotaur, a common figure in his paintings.

Unknown · *View of the Qumran Caves* · Israel Date Unknown Near the shores of the Dead Sea, ancient scrolls were discovered in caves of the biblical Judean desert in 1947. Finding the cave by chance, a shepherd uncovered clay jars containing 2000-year-old manuscripts.

Simon Quaglio
Astrofiammante, Queen of the Night, from Mozart's 'Magic Flute' · **Germany 1818** From the set design for the cherished and complex opera, drenched in masonic symbolism, the queen thunderously appears from a star-lined cave, clad in the night sky, riding on a crescent moon.

Todd Weaver
Photograph from the set of Move My Blood **United States · 2022** A photograph from *Move My Blood,* directed by Maximilla Lukacs and choreographed by Jennifer Rose. Shot inside Drogarati Cave in Kefalonia, Greece, the film explores the myth of the Goddess Circe through a theatrical dance performance.

(opposite) **Edward John Poynter** · *The Cave of the Storm Nymphs* · **England** · 1903 Underground, mythical grottoes were an ongoing theme in the artist's paintings. He captures the amusement and disregard of the sirens, languishing in their cave while sailors meet their demise.

(previous) **Nicholas Roerich** · *Most Sacred (Treasure of the Mountains)* · **Russia** · 1933 A painter, poet, mystic and crusader for peace, Roerich's expeditions to the Himalayas inspired his work. A sacred cavern of ceremonial beings amid crystals conveys the idea that the real treasures can be found within.

MOVEMENT
AS RITUAL

Festivals of the Spirit

Dance is the hidden language of the soul.

— MARTHA GRAHAM, Dancer & Choreographer, 1935

The pilgrim carves a path through holy lands, making a slow and ancestral passage through miles of road, all to pay homage at a chosen sacred site. The ancients dance at the altar, the village gathers in circles to celebrate the arrival of the spring, our bodies in the midst of movement are one of the oldest forms of all spiritual worship. Dance can be a method of praise in religious ceremonies and rituals, a way to express devotion, gratitude, and reverence to the goddess. In many cultures, dance is viewed as a way to connect directly with the divine or spiritual realms. Through movement, rhythm, and expression, dancers may seek to communicate with higher powers, deities, or ancestors, making the dance itself a form of prayer or offering.

In other traditions, the pilgrimage route is considered an ancient method of movement worship, the devoted traveling to those far-flung places considered most sacrosanct. There are numerous pilgrimage sites across the world that still hold significant religious and cultural importance. Among the most

renown pilgrim destinations is in Mecca, Saudi Arabia, home to the Kaaba, the most sacred site in Islam and destination for millions of Muslims who undertake the Hajj pilgrimage to Mecca each year. In India, the city of Varanasi, also known as Kashi, is one of the oldest continuously inhabited cities in the world and a prominent sacred site in Hinduism. Situated on the banks of the holy Ganges River, millions gather at Varanasi in veneration of the Hindu gods. In Tibet, a pilgrimage known as the Kailash Mansarovar Yatra takes place annually and revolves around Mount Kailash and Lake Mansarovar, a route significant in Hinduism, Buddhism, and Jainism. Lumbini, Nepal, considered to be the birthplace of Gautama Buddha, the founder of Buddhism, is another site that attracts Buddhist pilgrims from around the world who come to pay their respects at the sacred Mayadevi Temple. The Shikoku Pilgrimage is a Buddhist pilgrimage route which circles the island of Shikoku, Japan, and includes 88 temples associated with the monk Kūkai (also known as Kōbō Daishi).

Edward Steichen · *Isadora Duncan in The Parthenon*
Germany/United States · 1921 To Isadora Duncan, traveling to and dancing within the ancient Greek sites was a spiritual pilgrimage. Transfixed by the art,

architecture, and philosophy of the ancient tradition, her movement felt ecstatic in the Acropolis, merged with the spirit of the place.

The city of Jerusalem is considered a holy city in numerous spiritual traditions, including Judaism, Christianity, and Islam. Jerusalem is home to sites such as the Western Wall, the Church of the Holy Sepulchre and the Al-Aqsa Mosque. In Spain, Santiago de Compostela is the endpoint of the Camino de Santiago (Way of St. James), a pilgrimage route that has been followed by Christians for centuries. The Way of Saint Francis is a pilgrimage route in Italy which traces the path followed by Saint Francis of Assisi. This route starts in Florence and ends in Rome, passing through various towns associated with the saint's life.

Sacred movement and dance are also integrated into the worship of various religious traditions across cultures. The Sufi are known for their Whirling Dervishes dancers, who perform as both a form of meditation and devotion, spinning in whirling patterns in order to reach heightened spiritual states. Hula is a traditional Hawaiian dance form that encompasses both storytelling and spiritual expression, combining movements of the body, hands, and feet with chanting and music, often performed to honor deities or depict mythological tales. Bharatanatyam is a classical form of dance originating in the South Indian state of Tamil Nadu. It traces its roots to the ancient temples and is considered a form of prayer and an offering to the gods. The intricate footwork, expressive gestures, and hand movements make it a sacred and highly revered dance.

Eric Lafforgue · *Gabbra Tribe Woman Dance* · Kenya 2023 In the Chalbi Desert, Gabbra women dance at a gathering in Turkana Lake, Loiyangalani. The Gabbra are a Cushitic tribe of nomads living with and tending to herds of camels and goats in northern Kenya and the highlands of southern Ethiopia.

Michael P. Smith · *Larry Bannock, Big Chief, Golden Star Hunters* · United States · 1982 Known and trusted for his immersive and transcendent photos of cultural and spiritual events in New Orleans, the dance, chant, and ceremonial dress of the Mardi Gras Indians is captured in full spread.

In Africa, the Yoruba Egungun dances are an integral part of Yoruba religious and cultural practices. These dances involve masked performers embodying ancestral spirits, with the movements said to connect one with the spiritual realm. These dances are often performed during religious ceremonies and funerals, in order to pay respects to ancestors. In Tibetan Buddhism, Cham dances are vibrant and colorful masked dances performed by monks during various religious festivals. These dances depict Buddhist teachings, historical events, and mythological stories. Kathak is another classical spiritual dance form, originating in the temples of northern India and characterized by fast footwork, intricate rhythmic patterns, and storytelling through mime and gesture.

Dances also play a significant role within pagan rituals, celebrations, and ceremonies, often reflecting a deep connection to nature, the divine, and the spiritual beliefs of the practitioners. In many traditions, devout worship is shown in ritual and synchronized dances, such as young maidens circling around the wooden Maypole for instance, a practice which can be traced back to early

Ben Edge · *The Green Man of Bankside and October Plenty* · **England** · **2019** Edge paints a merged version of the green man in his roles in the twelfth night of Bankside, a new year's ceremony of mid-winter customs, and the harvest festival/bounty celebration during autumn.

Germanic and Celtic cultures. Thought to be a pre-Christian fertility rite practiced in the hopes of a successful harvest, this dance often occurs during Beltane, a Celtic festival celebrated on the first of May, which is also associated with the fire festival that marks the beginning of summer. Dancing around the Maypole, bonfire dances, and other celebrations are often part of Wiccan Beltane festivities.

Movement and dance remain a sacred form of expression. In the 20th century, the advent of modern dance transformed the rigid formality of ballet and other established dance styles. Pioneered by the American choreographer Martha Graham, modern dance is marked by innovative techniques and an expressive movement

style. Graham developed techniques that focused on the use of contraction and release to express emotions and ideas, her choreography often exploring themes of mythology, psychology, and the shared human experience. In the emotionally shattered post-War Japan of the 1950s, the avant-garde dance practice of Butoh was developed by choreographer Tatsumi Hijikata and dancer Kazuo Ohno. Touching on themes of darkness and transformation, Butoh often incorporates elements of ritual and improvisation into performances.

Movement is one of our most powerful ways to connect with each other and with our bodies. Through movement and expression, dancers seek spiritual healing, empowerment, and inner growth, using dance as a tool for

Bartolomeo Giuliano · *The Fairies (Le Villi)* · **Italy 1906** From the collection of Gallerie di Piazza Scala in Milano, Giuliano's classic evokes a mystical realm of mythology and fantasy, set below a moonlit sky with fairies and nymphs dancing upon the water.

Nicholas Kahn and Richard Selesnick · *The Lesson of the Maypole* · United States · 2019 From the series, "Madame Lulu's Book of Fate," the whimsically illustrated maypole characters dance, fully clothed in greenery.

Bihzad · *Dancing Dervishes, Folio from a Divan of Hafiz* · Iran · ca. 1480 The dance of the dervish is part of the Sufi mystic ceremony called Sema in which men transcend the ego through continual circular movement, inducing trance-like states to connect them with God.

(opposite) Marcella Blood · *The Maypole Dance* · United States 1920 What began as a fertility ritual, with young girls and boys dancing a woven tapestry of symbolic union and community, is still practiced according to varying customs all over the world. The artist chose to paint a ballroom, court rendition on copper plates with tempura.

(following) Joan Miró *The Harlequin's Carnival* Spain · 1925 A harlequin/guitar hybrid with a saddened expression and hole in his stomach may have been a metaphor for Miró's poverty-stricken state at the time of the painting. Rife with symbolism, he says the ladder is a symbol of flight, evasion, and elevation which defines the work as many of the objects seem to be in a state of movement.

The Halprin House Mountain Home Studio was a laboratory for movement and art research exploring this question of environment/ location/space as integral to the artistic process and to life itself. My grandmother, Ana Halprin, was part of the Fluxus Movement and explored how the material of our everyday lives and everyday movement was choreography for dance. My grandfather, Lawrence Halprin, was a designer. He built the Dance Deck and studio for my grandmother. It was the intersection of dance and design, a marriage of deep creative partnership. On that Dance Deck, dancers became explorers, non-dancers became dancers, non-artists became artists, poets sang, and musicians danced, and it was a blur of creation. Nature became the stage, rhythms of environment the ethos for artistic exploration. For my grandmother, who had put in her time in New York on Broadway and with Martha Graham, it was about getting off the stage and off the concept of proscenium arch as sanctified and into nature as sanctified, into body as sanctified. It was about how do we feel when we dance, and what can we transform and transmute through dance? Artist participants emerged transformed by movement, by inner realm meeting outer landscape, elucidated by art and environment as process. The Mountain Home Studio was a place of intention and attention and just stepping into the space opened a conduit. I'm interested in exploring this liminal space, the in-between, the transitional, in my own work. My time spent with my grandfather was my greatest education in this exploration. As a landscape architect he was in relationship to the liminal and how we transition through open space. He taught me to look deeply, to look at the details, to study nature and to look at its processes and then put it on a page, to find a way to document, interpret and express. My grandmother taught me to look inward, to feel, to feel the body in her core and to move, to move what needs moving and that its all material for art-making. Together, they taught me to activate those outward spaces and inward spaces and to see where these spaces might integrate, so that then we might return to seeing where we all connect.

— RUTHANNA HOPPER, Artist & Dancer, 2024

(opposite) Unknown
Butoh dance performance
Japan · Date Unknown
Themes of death and
dying are central in this
confrontational avant-
garde dance form.
Created by co-founders
Tatsumi Hijikata and
Kazuo Ohno in the late
1950s, this exploration
of modern movement
embraces the aftermath
of nuclear bombing and
the horror and grief of
a post-war Japan.

Laurie Lewis
Iphigenie auf Tauris
London · 2010 Pina
Bausch modernizes
the tragic Gluck opera
which takes place on
the Island of Tauris.
A king's daughter
and temple priestess,
Iphegenie takes pity on
two men captured by
the Goddess Diana.
As she attempts to free
them, she realizes one
of them is her brother.

Ron Wertheim
*Film Still from 'Invita-
tion to Lust'* · Holland
1968 With the aid
of an aphrodisiac, a
ritual, orgiastic cult
dance sequence creates
scientific discoveries in
the interest of humanity,
from the low budget
softcore director.

Tristram Kenton · *The Rite of Spring* · England 2008 The Pina Bausch Dance Theatre revives the 1913 Igor Stravinsky ballet for modern fans.

(following, top) John Lindquist · *Alvin Ailey at Jacob's Pillow* · United States · ca. 1961 Dancers Ted Shawn and Ruth St. Denis bought a retreat center in the Berkshires, ushering in a new era of dance and breaking down image barriers for men as dancers. They revolutionized dance in America by conceiving a multicultural model, challenging European ballet standards.

(following, bottom) Barbara Morgan *Martha Graham—Letter to the World (Kick)* United States · 1940 Having an intuitive understanding of dance as an "eloquent life force," Morgan aimed to promote hope by capturing the invigoration of the spirit through movement during the stress of the great depression. Graham's performance in the photo is based on the love life of poet Emily Dickinson.

Unknown · *Couple Dancing at the Savoy Ballroom*
United States · 1947 Considered the soul of the
neighborhood, the Harlem ballroom was a spectacle of sound and spirit in its heyday. Important was
the sense of place at the Savoy, where jazz music
and dance blossomed.

(following) Jacques Torregano · *Santeria* · France
1992 A parade of dancers honor the Orishas
Oshun and Yemaya, Goddesses of the Santeria
tradition, through dance and costume in Cuba.
Dancers embody the deities, believing that specific
movement induces communication.

Warner Jepson · *Anna Halprin's 'The Branch'*
United States · 1957 Just outside San Francisco, artist Halprin and her architect husband built a dance deck on their mountainside property which a branch sprouts up between the deck planks.

Basing her work on the "experience of sensation," bodies perform a choreographed dance and co-mingle with the branch and making use of the negative space between dancers and the outdoor sense of place.

Unknown · *Dancers wearing Kananga masks* Mali · 2006 The Dogon tribe of north and east Africa commemorate and honor the dead in the Dama ceremony wearing a mask symbolizing the kommolo tebu bird. The whole village participates in the celebration, displaying their own familial Kananga masks.

Tawaraya Sōtatsu *Bugaku Dance (detail)* Japan · 1630 Buddhist artist Sōtatsu, painter of paper screens and doors, portrays the dance drama traditionally performed only for the imperial court with accompanying gagaku music. Historical battles, mythology, and Buddhist storytelling define the dance.

Henri Matisse · *Dance*
France · ca. 1910
Dance is one of a
well-loved pair of
works commissioned
by Russian art patron,
Sergei Shchukin, in
which unconditional
joy is portrayed as
bodies join in liberating
and intuitive movement,
seemingly guided
by unconscious cosmic
force and free of
inhibition.

(opposite) Unknown
*Native American Hoop
Dancer* · United States
2000 As a symbol of
the circle of life and the
shape of the nucleus of
everything in life, Sioux
tribe member Jasmine
Pickner dances in the
tenth annual world
hoop dance champion-
ship in Phoenix, Arizona.
Dancers use up to
thirty hoops to pay
respect to the sacred-
ness of creation.

Unknown · *Lord Ganesh
Miniature Painting*
India · Date Unknown
Known as Dancing
Ganesha, the four-
armed elephant God
in happy dancing pose
bestows blessings to
the artist and is typically
invoked by devotees
before new projects
and endeavors.

Inatace Alphonse *Crowd Dancing* · Haiti 20th Century Throngs of Haitians dance in celebration through a winding street in the Alphonse oil on canvas. His work commonly depicted scenes of lively human interaction and positive exploration of community spirit.

PEREGRINACION.

Unknown · *Pilgrimage, from a history of the peregri-*
nations of the Syon Nuns · Portugal · 17th Century
Painted on vellum, this artwork depicts the pilgrim-
age route traversed by the Syon Nuns in Portugal.
This piece is currently in the collections at the Arundel
Castle in England.

Katsushika Hokusai
People Climbing the Mountain · Japan · 1830
From the series 'Thirty-Six Views of Mt. Fuji,' the woodblock depicts pilgrimage to the holy mountain, considered home to the divinities. Ascending the peak enables devotees to be cleansed of their transgressions.

Unknown · *Wailing Women* · Egypt ca. 1370 BCE
Grief-stricken, weeping women mourn the loss of the governor of Thebes, in a funeral procession scene painted on the wall of the tomb of Ramose in the Valley of the Nobles.

Min Wae Aung · *Towards Monastery-7* · Myanmar
2017 Buddhist monks' journey along the path to
their place of worship, leaving behind that which
causes humanity to suffer. In joy they process. Faces
of the monks are rarely shown as the artist conveys
cultural and spiritual aspects of his beloved country.

Lita Albuquerque · *Spine of the Earth* · United States
2012 Three hundred people in red formed a per-
formative sculpture of a spinal movement. The line
of performers walked down 287 stairs to mobilize
the spine and give it depth within the landscape.

TEMPLE
OF THE FLESH

Bowing to the Body

Hallow the body as a temple to comeliness and sanctify the heart as a sacrifice to love; love recompenses the adorers.

— KHALIL GIBRAN, from *The Prophet*, 2020

The body as temple, the devout worshipping at the altar of the womb, this is perhaps the most ancient of all spiritual practices. Sacred sites erected in honor of the gods of fertility, of birth and of the blossoming harvest, can be found in all parts of the globe, through prehistoric into pagan traditions, and in mythologies and religions around the world. The holy mother or the paternal provider, these are archetypes inherent within all facets of the shared human journey.

The Temple of Artemis at Ephesus, located in present-day Turkey, was dedicated to the Greek goddess Artemis, who was associated with childbirth and nature. In Egypt, the Temple of Isis at Philae, situated on an island in the Nile River, was devoted to the goddess Isis, known for her association with fertility, motherhood, and magic. Isis was often depicted as a potent symbol of feminine power and played a crucial role in ensuring the fertility of both the land and its people. For the Norse, Freyja, the goddess of love, was highly revered. She was also associated with

feminine fertility. Across the ocean, in what is now Mexico, the ancient Mesoamerican city of Teotihuacan features several structures thought to be linked to fertility symbolism. The Pyramid of the Moon and the Pyramid of the Sun are considered sacred sites associated with both fertility and agricultural rites. In Ecuador, the Cueva de los Tayos is believed to have been a sacred site for the area's indigenous tribes, featuring cave paintings and inscriptions related to fertility and agricultural practices.

In Hindu mythology, various deities are associated with both the body and regeneration. For example, the goddess Lakshmi is revered as the goddess of wealth, prosperity, and fertility. Tantra is a body-centric tradition originating in Hinduism and later adopted by various other belief systems. Tantra incorporates practices that honor and celebrate the body and sexuality. Some pagan practices emphasize this same connection, not only within the body but within the natural world as well, recognizing our physical bodies as an integral part of our connection to the earth.

Adelchi-Riccardo Mantovani · *Venus Genetrix*
Italy · 1996 Venus, as mother of all, is a frequent ancient temple dedication in many countries. Often depicted nude she is the embodiment of love and sexuality, a seductive divinity. The goddess born

from the sea in an oyster like a pearl was deemed a primary ancestor to the Romans. Mantovani's stylized version modernizes the sacred and symbolic cult of Venus.

VENVS   GENETRIX

(previous, left) Pan Yuliang · *Seated Nude Holding a Mirror* China · 1956 The female body symbolizes the birth of everything, seen and unseen. Celebration of women as the creative vessel of God and man, has been the subject of works of art regardless of criticism. Pan was widely appreciated as a nude and nature portraiture artist in the face of government disapproval.

(previous, right) Penny Slinger · *Rosebud* England/United States 1973 From her *Bride's Cake* series, the collage artist extraordinaire parodies the traditional wedding custom of cutting the cake. Radically departed from the conventional symbol of the ritual, a woman's body merged with the cake takes on a deeper meaning.

Meagan Boyd *Earthly Flesh* · United States · 2020 Illuminations of the human spirit abound in Boyd's ecstatic visions of earthly bodies in union with nature.

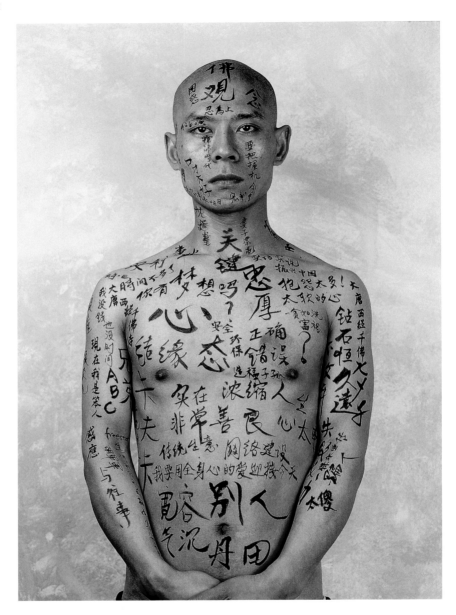

Zhang Huan · *1/2 (Text)* · China · 1998 As the
artist explains, "The body is the only direct way
through which I come to know society and society
comes to know me. The body is the proof of identity.
The body is language."

Marina Abramović · *Dozing Consciousness (Body)*
Serbia · 2016 Shot from her installation 'Spirit
House,' the performance artist endures extreme
bodily pain and exhaustion to define her limits and
demonstrate power, control, and spiritual capability.

(following) Théophile
Steinlen · *Massaida
on the Divan* · France
1912 The socialist art
nouveau painter had
many revered, exquisite
nudes, in addition to
anti-war posters, and
most notably—cat
paintings and sculp-
tures. He championed
bohemian themes while
being outspoken about
the ills of capitalism.

145

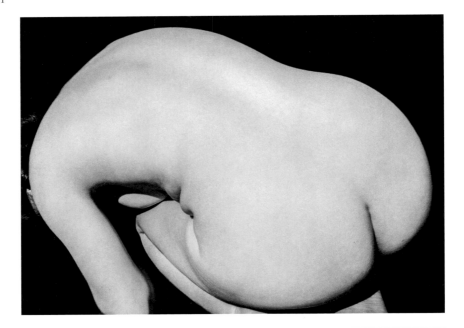

(top) Imogen Cunningham · *Nude* United States · 1932 Cunningham's nude photos attempt to de-sexualize the human body, capturing shapes void of the usual objectified parts. The contrasted photos put an easy lens on the flesh as an abstract art theme of the series.

(bottom) Egon Schiele · *Reclining Nude with Spread Legs* · Germany · 1914 The artist was imprisoned for a brief period for "making immoral drawings." His erotic and provocative art has influences of impressionism and art nouveau, with boldly added color to add intensity and focus to his organic drawings.

Vic Oh · *The Serpent Holder* · France · 2017 Through the passing phases of the moon, women channel the cosmos for their creative power, dark side, strength, and fire, as Oh conveys through the secretive messages within her art.

I don't believe that sacred space is different from mundane space. "Sacredness" is the accumulation of action and intention towards space: physical or abstract, exterior, or interior. The building up of this aim and effort over time creates tradition around specific spaces; thus arises the notion of a "sacred space." Often, we experience sacred space in nature too, in environments lightly or mostly untouched by human hands. It's these experiences that highlight the inherent sacredness of the material, of the manifested. The activation of space, actual or conceptual, is central to my artistic process. Whether it's the literal and symbolic space of an astrological chart or the space of the built environment or studio in a pendulum ritual, I'm always seeking out these seemingly prosaic spaces to highlight their inherent reality as spiritual. In my process, activation is less a tecÙology of transforming a space or channeling powers into a space than it is setting up the conditions to reveal what is already there and then simply getting out of the way. The sacred is there and ever-present, even if it doesn't match our ideals. I most resonate with the many centers and structures built by new religious movements of the 20th century, especially those in California. From the Integratron in the Mojave Desert to Krotona in the Hollywood Hills, these spiritual predecessors fought the headwinds of a skeptical materialism in their day to concretize sites dedicated to the evolving spirituality of humanity. Although the mystic knows the sacred is omnipresent, the Saturnian limitations of embodiment circumscribe what can be manifested in any one lifetime or era. The great effort represented by these sites are unassailable steps towards the re-enchantment of society and culture and their existence a lodestar towards what is possible. There is a theme in metaphysical discourse from antiquity to the present that the human is sacred spirit. I don't agree with the dualistic implications that many have historically drawn from this doctrine: that there is an essential sacred and profane, a higher and a lower, a Light and a Dark, high vibe and low vibe, etc. Instead, impossibly, paradoxically, it's all sacred. From the most horrific to the most transcendent, it's all one.

— **MICHAEL CARTER,** Metaphysician, Artist, & Educator, 2024

(opposite) Jean Le Noir
Wound of Christ
France · ca. 1345 From the medieval manuscript the 'Psalter and Prayer Book of Bonne de Luxembourg' comes a compelling image of the spear gash in the torso of Jesus, uncannily likened to the female vulva, which eroticized the body of Christ, emphasizing its nurturing and healing abilities. It perhaps unconsciously stimulated the viewer into further devotion.

Nous monstre tres dous dier me
trelguant largese.
Quant voulistes pour nous
louffrir tant de destrese.

Monica Sjöö · *Sheela Na Gig, Creation* · Sweden 1978 In eco-feminist symbolism, the creation of the world springs from the body of the great mother, the universal energy of conception. Sjöö unites nature, women, and animals into a whole, in the piece from her first ever solo exhibition.

(opposite) Koloman Moser · *Venus in the Grotto* · Austria · 1914 Appearing to exit a cave, Venus glimmers in gold as the goddess of love, beauty, and pro-creation, from one of the designers of the famed 'Ver Sacrum' journal. The cave might be a symbol of the "rebirth" of Venus as the morning star when she rises from darkness.

Leonor Fini · *Les etrangeres* · Argentina/ Italy · 1968 The Argentine-Italian painter was one of the key female artists of the Surrealist movement. Fini's work often focused on myths, eroticism, and the subconscious. "Paintings, like dreams, have a life of their own and I have always painted very much the way I dream," she once said.

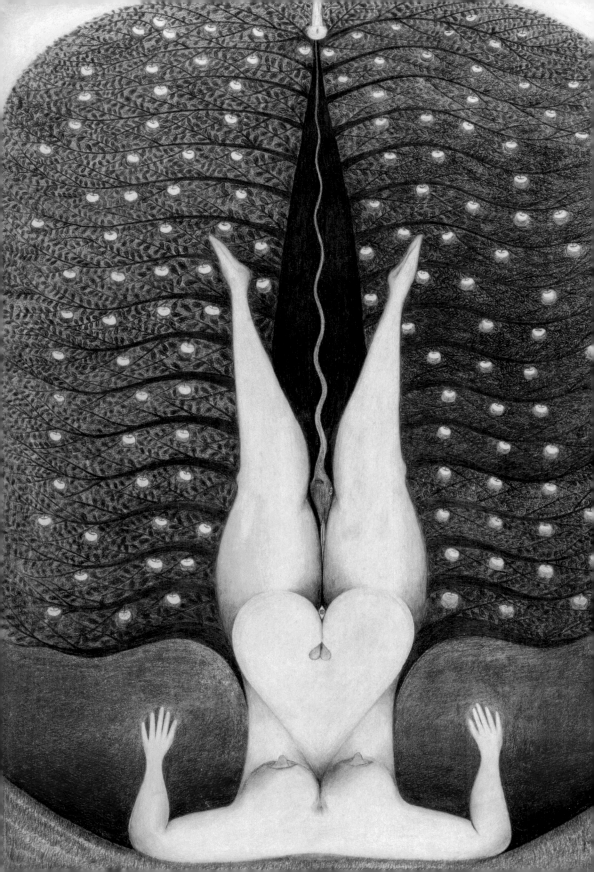

(following pages)
Leonor Fini · *Chthonian Deity Watching over the Sleep of a Young Man* Argentina/Italy · 1946 In her perpetual opposition to masculine domination of art, and especially the surrealist scene, Fini offers matriarchal visions. The underworld sphinx-like creature, possibly a Hecate connection, bears the usual likeness to the artist.

Friedrich Schröder-Sonnenstern · *Praxis* · Germany 1952 Known for his fantastical art, Schröder-Sonnenstern was often a misunderstood victim of psychiatric confinement.

Herbert List · *Youth and Roman Bust* · Germany 1949 Swiss painter Rolf Dürig is the subject in List's thematic photo recalling the Pygmalion myth.

(top) Unknown · *Erotic Miniature* · India 19th Century Indians had a thoughtful view of erotic reality, recognizing the pursuit of pleasure as essential to life itself and crucial to eventual enlightenment. The adoration and beautification of sexual organs and positions was highly popularized through the Ancient Hindu *Kama Sutra* text.

Unknown · *Chinese erotica painting* · China · 19th Century From the late Qing dynasty, one of a rare series of paintings is meant as a tender, loving and humorous depiction of sexuality. Erotic art from this time was mostly destroyed during the Maoist cultural revolution.

(bottom) Unknown · *Farewells of Abu-Zayd and Al-Harith before the return to Mecca* · Iran · 13th Century An exquisitely inscribed and illustrated image from a rare, illuminated manuscript.

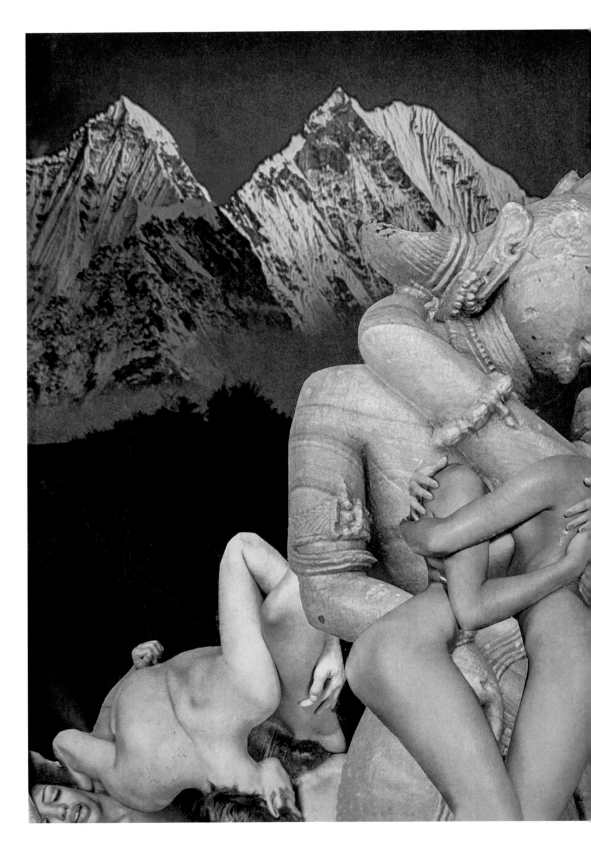

Penny Slinger · *Tantric Reunions* · England/ United States · 1976 Creating "a language for the feminine psyche to express itself," the collage artist shows her Tantric influence, merging sacred sensuality with mysticism in her surrealist style.

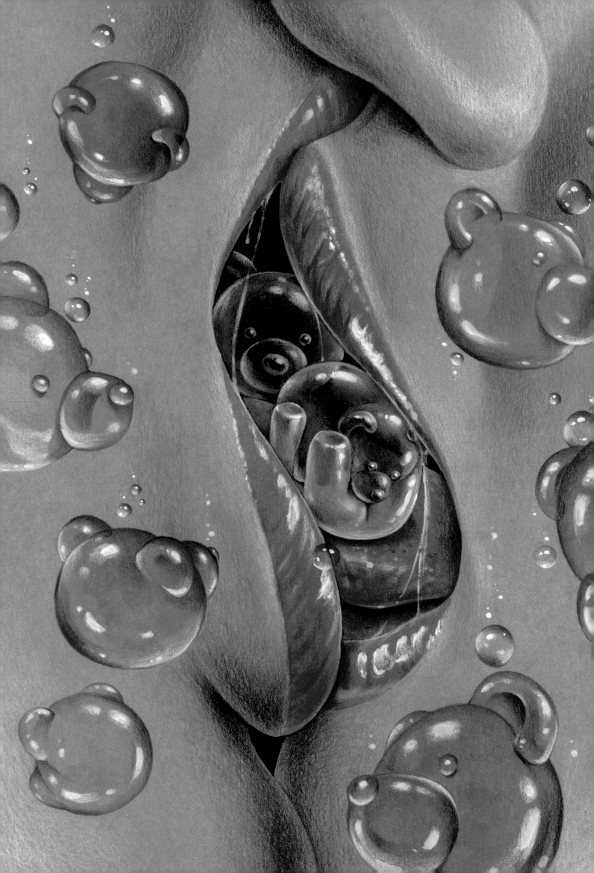

Joyce Lee · *Jelly Dream 3* · South Korea · 2023
Erotic pop surrealism in a delectable gummy bear
kiss, with the most luscious lip and candy colors,
both tantalizes and incites joy. Lee prefers to express
human emotion thoughtfully as a fun visual sugges-
tion—leaning into eroticism without trepidation.

Alphachanneling · *Queen of the Forest* · United
States · 2021 As the artist explains, "Does your
heart overflow with gratitude for the mysteries of
creation? Let the Queen of the Forest teach you
how to celebrate all that is beautiful within and
around you."

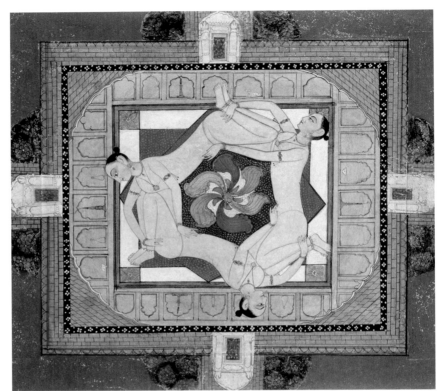

Unknown · *Tantric miniature depicting three women forming a chain* India · 19th Century Within a mandala forming geometric shapes with a floral center, three nude women form a chain of light caressing, suggesting foreplay. Tender facial expressions keep the imagery soft and natural, as is a prevalent depiction in erotic Indian art.

Unknown · *Erotic Scene* Italy · 1st Century The Augustan Villa of the Farnesina was discovered in Trastevere in 1879. Before its destruction, the impeccable erotic and mythological frescoes were removed and eventually installed in Palazzo Massimo alle terme.

Virgo Paraiso · *Return to Paradise* · Mexico · 2002
As the artist explains in a statement regarding their
work, "Return to Paradise depicts the moment of
awakening to the realization that you are the source
of existence, the fountain of love, joy, beauty, serenity,
and divine wisdom that gives life to everything in the
universe and beyond."

(opposite)
Hildegard Von Bingen
*The Cosmic Sphere and
Human Being* · Germany
12th Century The
great German mystic,
Saint Hildegard, wrote
several works on her
visionary theology, one
being *The Book of
Divine Works*. From the
"voice of God" in celes-
tial, layered wheels, the
image overflows with
symbolism of the cosmic
reality contained within
the human experience.

(following, left)
Salvador Dalí · *Dalí,
nude, entranced in the
contemplation of five regu-
lar bodies metamorphosed
in corpuscles, in which
suddenly appears Leonardo's
"Leda," chromosomatised
by the face of Gala* · Spain
1954 Replete with
symbolism, Dalí paints
himself nude with his
manhood hidden by
a hard shell, kneeling
on a soft stingray, in
a messianic posture
beholding an almost
unattainable Gala in
highly genetic form.

The key actions in my work are my body, the sculptures I make, and the Earth, all working together in front of the camera. Given how long the exposures are in my work, a minimum of 15 minutes, my process has more in common with experimental film than still photography. Through each photograph, time compresses. Within that time, a performance is made for the camera, a collaboration of light and movement. Ultimately, my work questions how our existence on Earth is bent, folded, and slipped into Earth's total existence, offering speculative futures, unimaginable pasts, and an anxious present. In my series titled Bronson Caves, *the cinematic and, therefore, representational history of the caves are woven into the narrative. The caves are in Los Angeles' Griffith Park and are famous as filming locations for countless motion pictures and television shows. With each cinematic event, the landscape's existence morphs and adapts to new realities, an asteroid colony one event, a vampire lair the next. In my most recent series titled* How Close, *the work was made at Red Rock Canyon in the Mojave Desert of California. In all its sublime beauty, the site exists restlessly in the present despite its ability to easily represent different places and moments in time. For example, it was the set of the movie Jurassic Park, has been the rightful home of the Indigenous Kawaiisu Peoples for 1500 years, and currently supports a critical aqueduct to Los Angeles. 250 million years ago it was the floor of the Pacific Ocean. I first saw Red Rock 10 years ago while driving through the Mojave. Fluted red walls quickly enveloped my view; the Earth lifted skyward at dynamic angles, confounding any sense of scale. Years later, after much change, I returned to the canyon to seek what I had felt: a deep connection to existence immersed in time. Being at the site of an ancient landscape, the sacred fills my experience, ironically during a moment when our presence is causing the most change to Earth's systems.*

— BRYCE BISCHOFF, Artist, 2024

(following, right top) Unknown · *Erotic sculptures
of loving couples at Lakshmana temple, Khajuraho,
Madhya Pradesh* · India · 930–50 Built by Chandela
kings on their sacred temple, the erotic scenes of a
tantric nature were common in Khajuraho as women
were considered divine.

(following, right bottom) Unknown · *Penis
Parinirvana* · Japan · 19th Century Women with
faces shaped like vulvas lament the passing of a
penis body in a scroll that parodies the classic image
of Buddha's sacred death. Meant to be playful,
erotic art, known as Shunga, was popular in Japan.

Louise Bourgeois · *Eyes* France/United States 1995 An ingenious title for what are clearly large breasts in Oslo's Tjuvholmen Sculpture Park, the sculptor had a penchant for provocative statements that stood in the face of patriarchal convention.

Unknown · *Delos, Colossal Phallus* · Greece 300 BCE Dedicated to Dionysus and symbolizing life force energy, penis statues stand erect on Delos Island, one of the most important historical, religious, and mythological sites in the ancient world.

(opposite) Pablo Picasso *Le Phallus* · Spain 1903 Contrasting the fundamental male and female dichotomy through a rigid and straight-faced penis and a soft and graceful female form. Picasso finesses the energies inherent in the pairs of opposites.

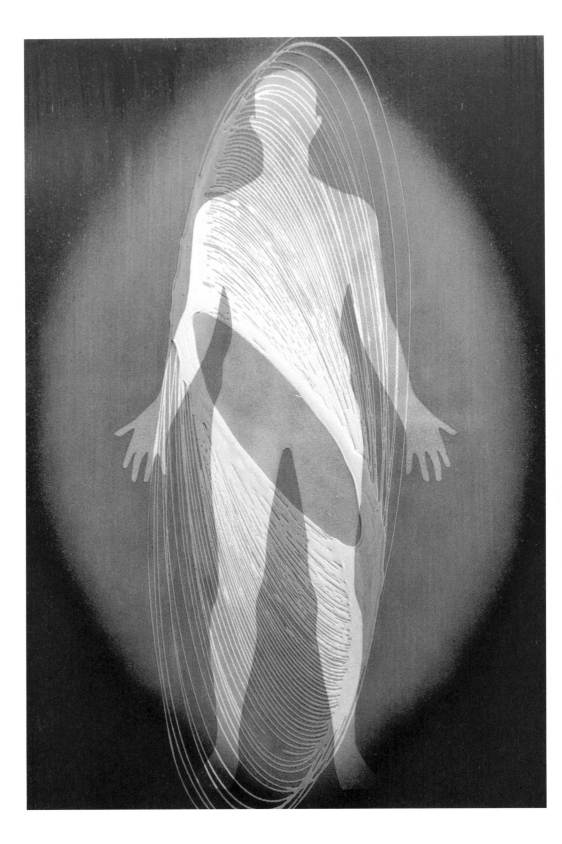

(previous)
David Black · *Swimmers*
United States · **2022**
International fashion
magazine, *Numero*,
published issue 239
in honor of the element
water. David Black
photographed nude
bodies in deep,
dark water, capturing
light reflections like
a starry sky.

(opposite) **Michael Carter** · *Energy Body* · **United States** · **2021** Using a pendulum of paint, the artist senses and simulates the vibrations emanating from the body to create the diagram of the subject's energy field.

Magdalena Wosinska · *With In* · **United States** 2019 The feminine form, as embodied by the artist, is a primary theme in the work of the Polish American, California-based photographer. Wosinska creates an ongoing series of self-portraits, posing in remote and stunning landscapes around the globe.

Pierre et Gilles
Mercure, Enzo junior
France · 2001
The caduceus, staff of
Hermes, is touching
down to the ground in
the photo of the nude,
wing-capped God,
Mercury, by a duo
of artists who shoot
mythological scenes,
film icons, and symbolic
figures of lore.

Giambologna
Appennine Colossus
Italy · 16th Century
Both a guardian of
earth and becoming
one with it, the gentle
giant was once one
of many bronze
sculptures in the park
of Villa Demidoff. He
now stands alone as
evidence of his sacred
connection to nature.

Jacques Le Moyne · *A Young Daughter of the Picts*
France · 1585–88 Early inhabitants of the British
Isles, the Picts, were a group of people who lived in
what is now Scotland during the Late Iron Age and
Early Medieval periods.

Niki de Saint Phalle and Larry Rivers · *Clarice
Rivers* · France/United States · 1964 Inspired
by a pregnant friend, Phalle created her first
"Nana" sculpture to invert the perception of women
as child-bearing sex objects.

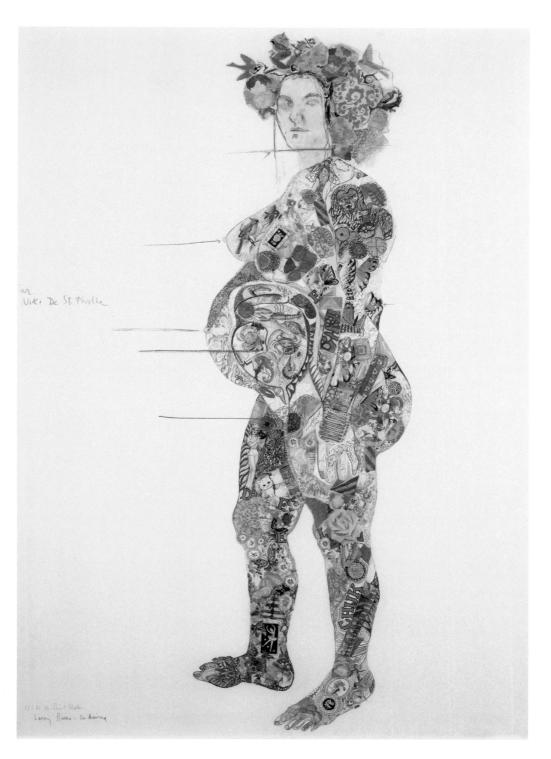

Par
Niki De St Phalle

Niki de Saint Phalle
Larry Rivers — En dessinant

Unknown · *Four-armed Avalokitesvara (Guanyin) Goddess of Mercy* China/Tibet · 20th Century The Tibetan representation of the Chinese Goddess of compassion, Kuan Yin, sits in symbolic repose as a Bodhisattva— enlightened beings who choose to serve, assist, and protect human-kind once attaining realization.

Hazel Florez *The Spiral Path* England · 2020 Humans are intrinsically connected to nature's rhythms of change— cyclical and spiralic. We are ever-evolving as alchemical beings. Esoteric surrealist, Florez depicts the vessel of philosophical lore with various symbolic elements.

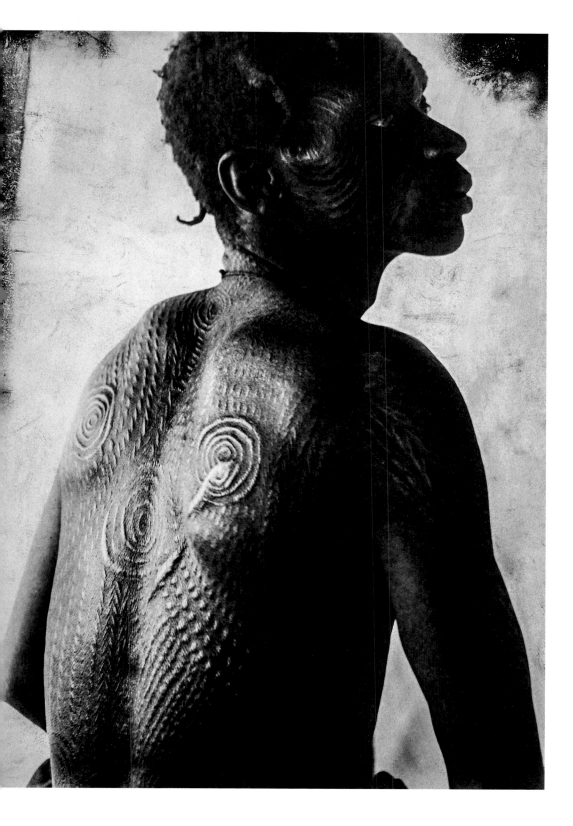

(previous, left)
Patricia A. Schwimmer
*Life Among the Mush-
rooms* · Canada · 1994
Exploring the sacred in
their work, Schwimmer
delves into a vivid
depiction of the body of
life-giver and nurture,
mother as archetype of
earth and nature.

(previous, right)
Emil Torday · *Man,
Congo (gelatin silver
print)* · Hungary · 1919
In an image featured
in an early edition of
National Geographic
magazine, a man from
the Democratic Republic
of the Congo proudly
displays his sacred tribal
scars.

Nicholas Roerich · *Mother of the World* · Russia
1924 The ancient, archetypal Great Mother atop the
mountains as her throne, serves humanity as life-
giver, protector, judge, and discerner of the polarity
of opposites, including light and darkness. Her veil
invokes the primal nature of her being—unmanifest.

Kailash Raj · *Kundalini Yoga Chakras in Human
Body* · India · Date Unknown The serpent force
that lies dormant at the base of the spine, known
as Kundalini, rises through wheels of energy
located along the spine in an invisible dimension
of the body.

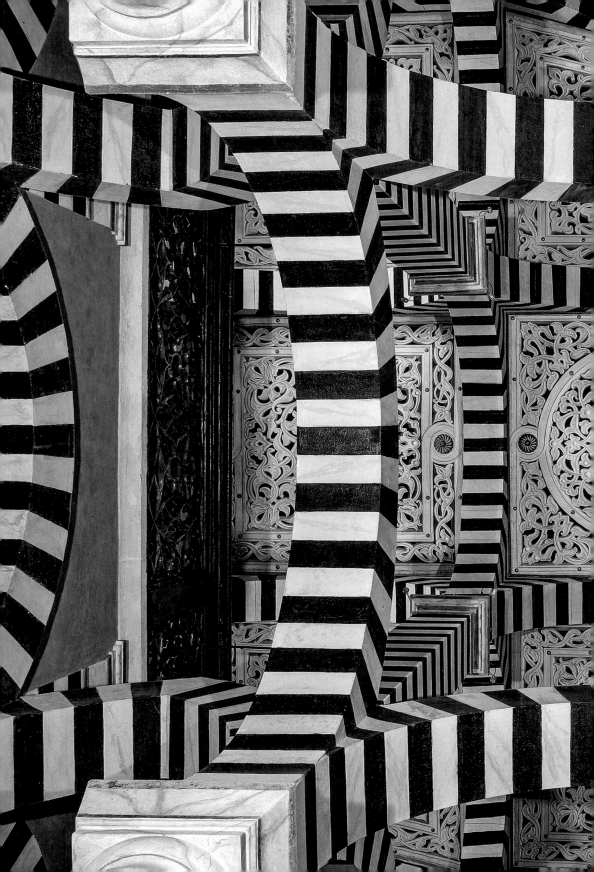

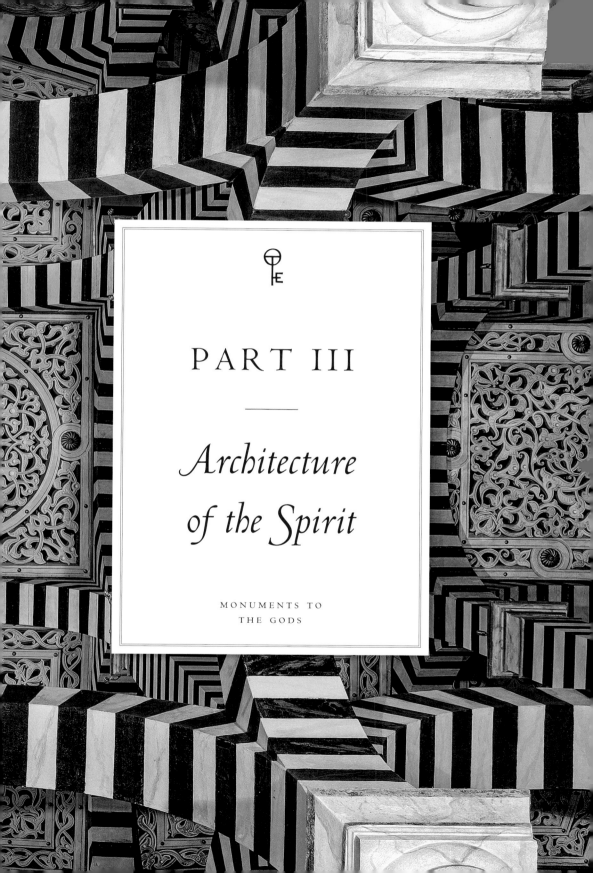

PART III

Architecture of the Spirit

MONUMENTS TO
THE GODS

PART III

UPON THE ALTAR

Elements of Ritualistic Symbolism

When the human race learns to read the language of symbolism, a great veil will fall from the eyes of men.

— MANLY P. HALL, Philosopher & Seeker, from *The Secret Teachings of All Ages*, 1928

The Christian cross, the Star of David in Judaism or the Taoist Yin and Yang, representing the balance of opposing forces in the universe—throughout the world, religious architecture often incorporates symbols aligned with specific faiths and beliefs, each with their own significant cultural and spiritual meanings.

The cross is perhaps the most well-known of these symbols, central to Christianity and representing Christ's sacrifice and salvation. The design of the cross can vary between different Christian sects, with some using more elaborate designs and others preferring simplicity. In Catholicism, for example, the crucifix is a common symbol that features a representation of Jesus on the cross. In Judaism, The Star of David is one of the most sacred symbols and is often used in synagogue architecture around the globe. The six-pointed star represents the connection between God and the Jewish people, as well as the unity of all Jews around the world.

In Taoism, the Yin and Yang symbol can be seen in various forms in Taoist temples and architecture, often alongside depictions of dragons and other mythical creatures. In Buddhism, the symbolism of The Wheel is often used in the design of temples and other religious structures, representing the teachings of the Buddha and the journey of reaching enlightenment, as well as the interconnectedness of all living things in the universe. The design of the wheel can vary between different Buddhist sects, but it often includes a central hub with spokes radiating outwards. In Islamic culture, the Crescent Moon is often used in the design of mosques. The symbol represents both the new moon, which for many Muslims signals the beginning of a new sacred month, and the star, which represents the light of knowledge and guidance. The use of this symbol in architecture has become particularly prominent in the Islamic Ottoman Empire, where it was incorporated into the design of many of its most iconic mosques.

In early pagan and indigenous practices, symbols were often inspired by the natural and animal realms—the sacred bull of the ancient

Unknown · *Rocchetta Mattei Chapel* · Italy 19th Century Located in the northern Apennines, the fantastic fortress is styled in a merging of many architectures. The chapel with the striped ceiling mimics the Cordoba cathedral in Spain and houses the body of Mattei, inventor of electrohomeopathy, in a buried sarcophagus. A lion, hippogriff, and harpies guard the entrance where astrological and esoteric symbols are endless.

(opposite) **Unknown · *The Divine Eye of Caodaism* Vietnam · 20th Century** Established in 1926, the Cao Dai syncretic religion in Vietnam holds that all religions are equal and convey the same message.

An all-seeing left eye is framed in a triangle surrounded by rays and lotus blossoms in the Holy Cao Dai temple at Tay Ninh.

Minoans, the oak tree worshipped in Celtic and Nordic ritual, and the pinecone in Greece, Rome, and Egypt which symbolized fertility and immortality. In esoteric teachings, the pinecone is also often associated with awakening and the expansion of consciousness. It is believed to represent the pineal gland, a small gland in the brain considered by some spiritual traditions to be the "third eye" or the seat of spiritual insight.

Unknown · *Cernunnos* · Denmark · 1st Century Forged in metal in the late Iron Age, the mysterious Gundestrup cauldron was found in a bog in Denmark and reveals images that would have been unknown to the people of the area, featuring the Celtic God of nature, flora, fauna, and fertility.

Thomas Pennant · *The Wicker Man of the Druids* **Wales · ca. 1776** A wicker man is set afire in the illustrated *A Tour in Wales* by Pennant. These pagan effigies were created to be burned as a symbol for purification, inner change, and transformation; a purging of the past to make space for renewal.

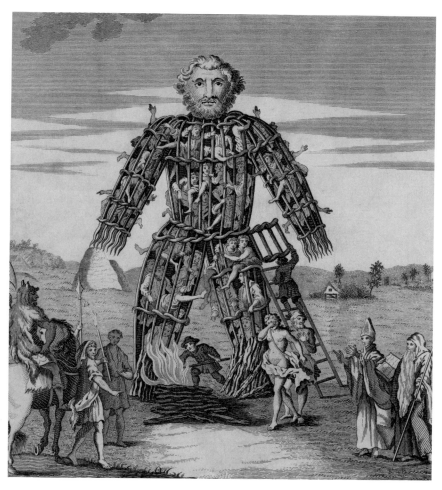

Perhaps the most well-known of these ancient symbols is the Egyptian ankh, also called the Key of Life or the Egyptian Cross. One of the most recognizable and widely used symbols in Egyptian art and religion, the Ankh is thought to symbolize life, fertility, and eternal existence. Most often depicted as a looped cross, the vertical line is said to represent the path of the sun, and the horizontal line, the horizon, or the earthly plane. In ancient Egypt, the ankh was closely associated with the gods and goddesses, particularly those connected to fertility and the afterlife—the divine power to give and sustain life.

*What is sacred? Some of the most typical ways for us to imagine the
sacred is when we're awestruck out in nature and quite accurately over-
whelmed with feelings of awe at these specific areas of the world. Modern
sacred spaces are often creative or cultural spaces, spaces for catharsis.
The Burning Man Festival, for instance, is sacred space which culminates
in the burn of structure, a moment that highlights the impermanence
of things. And typically, inside the temples at Burning Man, there are
also spaces for memorials. People leave names of their lost loved ones
inside the structure and on the last night of the festival, there is 'the burn'.
Sacred space is something that humans continue to create. Areas become
sacred sites when people ascend them and revere them and honor them
as sacred. These sacred spaces are also repositories of the tradition which
created them. Often, sacred spaces are built in relationship to a natural
geography that is meaningful somehow, a mountaintop or by a river, or
atop an ancient pagan sacred site or temple. The first sacred space was
the cave. The cave served as shelter but also, as a womb, an earth womb.
From the cave, you then have the worship of nature and then the creation
of sacred symbolic architectural forms as well. You've got the sphere, the
spiral, the pyramidal form, the labyrinth. And these sacred architectures
appear all over the world. Yet in some ways, every sacred space returns
to that original idea of the cave as the womb, as a space for the gestation
of the awakening of human spirit.*

— ALLISON GREY & ALEX GREY, Artists & Seekers, 2024

Unknown · *Chartres Cathedral Labyrinth* · France
1194–1250 Situated above an earth energy source,
the gothic cathedral with its grotto-filled crypts and
a sacred spring, has one of France's largest labyrinths. It marks the very nave of the edifice and
takes around 30 minutes to traverse.

Francisco De Goya
*Adoration of the Name of
God* · Spain · 1771–72
Angels cluster around
the glowing triangle in
an initial sketch for a
fresco Goya painted
on the ceiling above
the Small Choir of the
Virgin in the Basílica de
Nuestra Señora del Pilar
in Zaragoza. The Tetra-
grammaton, or *YHWH*
was painted within the
golden triangle in the
final version.

Herbrandt Jamsthaler
*Illustration from
Viatorium Spagyricum*
Germany · ca. 1622
Perfect union of body,
mind, and spirit—the
enlightened state,
also known as the
philosopher's stone, is
esoterically instructed
through the science of
alchemy, and illustrated
through highly symbolic,
magickal imagery.

Donato Bramante · *The Belvedere Courtyard, Vatican
Palace* · Italy · 16th Century Originally a first century statue at the Temple of Isis, later moved to Vatican City, the bronze pinecone is placed center stage
in the courtyard. It has long been a pagan symbol
of fertility, and more esoterically represents the
pineal gland or third eye, our connection point
between the physical and spiritual worlds.

(following) Unknown *Telesterion in Eleusis* Greece · 5th–4th Centuries BCE As an initiation ceremony hall for the Eleusian mysteries, the Telesterion contained a shrine to Demeter, Goddess of nature and her daughter, Kore. Now in ruins, the sacred site served as a center of spiritual importance, remaining so today.

(opposite) Stefan Ziese · *Lower Saxony* · Germany 2021 Geometrically shaped Star of David memorial to murdered Jews marks the site where the Goettingen Synagogue, which was destroyed by Nazi's, once stood.

(top) Unknown · *Wolleka Falasha Jewish Village* Ethiopia · 20th Century Kept intact by current Ethiopian residents is the small village once populated by Jews who lived secretly for a few generations in the area.

(bottom) Unknown · *Ethiopian Synagogue in Acre* Ethiopia · 20th Century Religious persecution caused Jews in Ethiopia to live clandestine lives and build secret synagogues in rural areas. Small communities lived for centuries in secret yet practiced their faith.

Unknown · *Lararium* · Italy · 1st Century Within
the stone city of Pompeii, in the House of the Vettii,
a preserved shrine to the guardian spirits of the
Roman household stands unscathed by the volcanic
destruction. It depicts a snake, to be worshiped for
the land's fertility and prosperity.

Unknown · *Altar at the Phuoc An pagoda* · Vietnam
Date Unknown In this modern Buddhist temple,
an altar is decorated with both ancient Buddhist
symbols and neon light details.

John Yarker · *Illustration from "The Kneph"* · England ca. 1884 An illustration from, "The Kneph" a "Gazette of Freemasonry and Masonic Rituals," depicts various symbols of the Free Masonry—the Serpent Ouroboros, the Delta or Divine Triangle, and the divine eye with the sun.

Unknown · *Modal Ankh* · Egypt · 1981–1802 BCE The 'key of life' hieroglyph, was representative of eternal life in Ancient Egypt, often found in tombs to honor the everlasting life, including death and reincarnation of the "ka," or soul.

*Architect Keith Critchlow described Chartes Cathedral and oth-
er sacred architecture as spaces that connect us to egolessness and
timelessness. They are physical spaces where we can connect to the
unitive state of consciousness through shared wonder and awe. They
are spaces where we connect with our own inner divinity, where we
feel connected to something much greater than ourselves. My work
reinterprets sacred spaces found in my own life, places of deep peace
and connection. Using VR technology and field recordings from the
icebergs of Antarctica, the beaches of Malibu, the lakes of Northern
Minnesota, and the flower fields of Carlsbad, I captured the moments
and spaces where I experienced intense unity. I create digital sacred
spaces for people to connect to non-egoic states of consciousness through
wonder, awe, and fascination. I use the structure of an immersive
mixtape to guide users through their experience. Each song and visual
world represents a sacred space, and a stage in the journey of transcendence from ego. Each section features real world light remixed into
kaleidoscopic worlds, whether that's the seas of Antarctica or massive
laser and mirror sculptures. I remix light, color, and sound along
with curated narratives to guide the users to and through the unitive
state. These aren't just visionary experiences; they're tools for actively
engaging with the same consciousness achieved in physical sacred
spaces. We urgently need to protect our shared physical sacred spaces
and we need to continue to build and nurture new sacred spaces and
experiences, whether that's in the real world at festivals like Burning
Man or Glastonbury, or virtual sacred spaces like I am building. It's
essential right now that we cherish systems and places that can help
us break out of our constant state of fight or flight. At a time when it
feels like every screen is designed and personally-customized to trigger
ego, anxiety, fear, and impulse, we need to cherish and champion things
that can remind us that we are more than our physical bodies, and a
collection of impulses and reactions. Sacred sites bring us together with
shared wonder and connection.*

— CHRIS HOLMES, Artist, Musician, & Seeker, 2024

(opposite)
David Roberts
*An Entranceway at
Karnak* · Scotland
1864 Among the many
temples near the banks
of the Egyptian Nile,
built and rebuilt by
successive pharaohs,
the walls, and the shafts
of the columns of the
Hypostyle Hall were
covered with reliefs and
inscriptions showing
adoration of the deities.

(following) Nicolas Poussin · *The Adoration of the Golden Calf* France · 1633–34 One of a pair of biblical paintings, a scene of the Israelites worshipping the golden calf representing God's power for having delivered the Israelites from Egypt, took place during the exodus and Moses' famous journey up Mount Sinai.

Unknown · *Full moon on Persepolis* · Iran ca. 550–330 BCE The sun rises on the eastern Gate of the Nations, also known as the Gate of Xerxes, King of the Achaemenid Empire. Flanked by Lamasu protection deities, the inscription reads: "A great god is Ahuramazda, who created this earth, who created heaven, who created man, who created happiness for man, who made Xerxes king."

(opposite) František Rint · *Entrance at Sedlec Ossuary* · Czech Republic · 1870 Sedlec Ossuary, Church of All Saints in Kutna Hora is decorated with the bones of up to seventy-thousand skeletons, exumed and utilized to make room for more. Due to its unique architecture, it has been deemed a World Heritage Site.

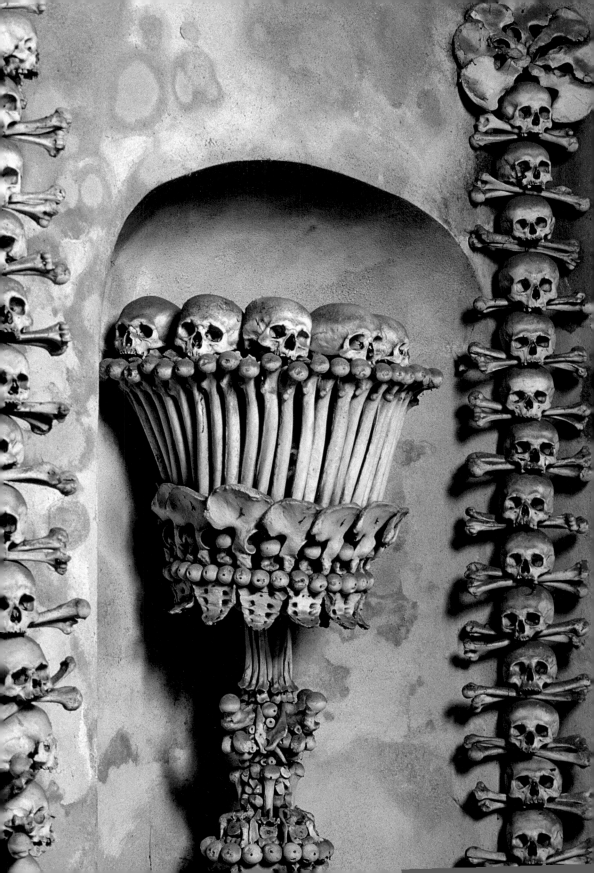

(following pages)
Unknown · *Pergamon Altar of Zeus and Athena* Greece · 180–160 BCE Using the golden ratio in their architecture, ancient Greeks built the acropolis to signify triumph over chaos. It contains a frieze with relief sculptures depicting the mythological battle known as Gigantomachy, the fight between the Gods and the titans, and included an altar for the practice of religious, animal sacrifices. It was excavated in 1878 and installed in a German museum.

Theodore Edaakie · *Zuni - Altar* · United States 1945 The Zuni artist Edaakie often depicted his indigenous Zuni culture in his work, such as this representation of a Zuni altar at the Pueblo Zuni Reservation in McKinley County, New Mexico.

Carl Gustav Carus · *Goethe Monument* · Germany 1832 An imagined sarcophagus bearing the remains of Johann Wolfgang von Goethe rests amid a dark, rocky terrain as a sacred space of pilgrimage. Carus gave him holy status in the painting as the artists both greatly admired each other's work.

Unknown · *The Goddess Selket on the Canopic Shrine from the Tomb of Tutankhamun* · Egypt · 1370–1352 BCE Selket, the Goddess of healing, is enshrined in gilded wood with a scorpion headdress and once stood as protector of the alabaster chest holding the internal organs of the boy Pharaoh, Tutankhamun.

Unknown · *Naga Stone Sculpture Guarding the Buddhist Temple of Ho Phra Keo* · Laos · 1565–66 Nagas, sacred serpent deities, guard the temple that once held the famed Emerald Buddha statue.

AS ABOVE, SO BELOW

Cornerstones of Mystical Architecture

True religion is universal: Christ, Buddha or Mohammed, the name means little, for we recognize only the light and not the bearer. We worship at every shrine, bow before every altar, whether in temple, mosque, or cathedral, realizing with our truer understanding, the oneness of all spiritual truth.

— MANLY P. HALL, Philosopher & Seeker, from *The Secret Teachings of All Ages*, 1928

We pay homage to the heavens with our sacred architecture, our worship of the gods and goddesses above manifested in majestic structures of rock and wood, glass and steel. Each religious practice features an accompanying approach to architecture—be it gilded domes, buttressed ceilings, intricate stained glass, vibrant murals, or elaborate gardens. Yet even at the very early stages of our spiritual expression, we have been transforming space. From the mysterious ancient artworks our ancestors painted upon cave wall, to the soaring cathedral towers, our human-constructed sacred sites highlight our elaborate and diverse ways of paying homage to the divine.

We have been building sacrosanct spaces since time immemorial, with the earliest dating back tens of thousands of years. In pagan and prehistoric cultures, one of the most famous sacred places is Göbekli Tepe in Turkey, estimated to be over 11,000 years old. The area consists of multiple stone circles and T-shaped pillars, indicating what is believed to be some form of ritual or ceremonial significance. Other examples of early sacred sites include the Neolithic stone circles such as Stonehenge in England and the megalithic structures found in various parts of the world.

Among the major global religions, some of the earliest known sacred sites include the Hindu Mundeshwari Temple in India, believed to have been built around the 5th century, although some sources suggest it may be even older. The earliest Christian church building is believed to be the Dura-Europos church in Syria, which is estimated to have been built in the 3rd century. The oldest mosque still in existence is the Quba Mosque in Medina, Saudi Arabia, believed to have been built by the Islamic prophet Muhammad in the year 622.

Throughout all sacred structures, the desire to connect with spirit is matched by our innate human need to connect with each other, our enduring desire for gathering and community. Even within the isolation of the hermitage or monastery there are nearly always spaces in which worshippers are meant to come together in union, to sit or to dance, in meditation, in prayer, and in song.

Apollo 8 Spacecraft · *Earth and Moon: Earthrise* Outer Space · 1968 Just as the moon rises when earthbound, the Apollo 8 crew were awarded the view of the earth rising as they orbited the moon from their control module. A sacred sight of never-seen-before proportions by the first, non-landing, human mission to the moon.

ELEMENT
Water

ENERGY
Vastness
The Expanse

NOTE
C#

FIRE AND ROCK

Image in Nature
WATER

COLOR
Black

MATERIALS
Pigment

CARDINAL DIRECTION
North

Fire and Rock

We're made for the light of a cave and for twilight. Twilight is the time we see best. When we dim the light down, and the pupil opens, feeling comes out of the eye like touch. Then you really can feel color and experience it.

— JAMES TURRELL, Artist, from an interview with *The Financial Times*, 2013

The earliest sacred sites were perhaps those which also offered shelter, protection from the elements or from wild beasts, deeply carved rock lairs which remained miraculously dry amid storms and resonated with warmth from family and fire. It is on these ancient walls of stone that our ancestors etched and painted their spiritual stories, from the shapes of animals which provided survival, meat and pelts, or the outlines of human hands, impressed upon the rock, ghostly remnants of tribal gatherings.

In the rugged sandstone cliffs of Australia there is sacred art believed to have been painted a millennia ago. Dating back as far as 40,000 years, these images are older than the pyramids, older than Stonehenge, and represent what are known as, "Dreaming" stories by the area's Aboriginal peoples, art describing the creation of the world itself and all the forces that animate it. In France, deep within the Lascaux Caves, some of the most iconic examples of prehistoric art survives. Discovered in 1940, these caves contain paintings of animals, as well as abstract shapes, and symbols, many estimated to be over 17,000 years old. At Altamira Cave, in Spain, similar paintings, which are believed to be around 14,000 years old, include images of bison, horses, and other animals.

Within the Bhimbetka Rock Shelters, in India, is art dating as far as 30,000 years, depicting everything from scenes of hunting to the essential rituals of everyday life. In the Tsodilo Hills in Botswana, Africa, rocks feature over 4000 individual ancient paintings across various sites. The Côa Valley in Portugal contains thousands of petroglyphs, dating back to the Upper Paleolithic era, approximately 22,000 to 10,000 years ago.

Across the globe, our ancestors felt the pull to create, to memorialize, to document and perhaps, to worship. In the glow of flames, they traced their narratives and praised their gods—leaving us with ancient symbols of our lasting connection to nature, to plants and to animals, to the skies high above, and to the grounds below.

(previous page) Unknown · *Two Men with Wolf Masks* · Algeria · 7000–6000 BCE Located in caves in the "Plateau of Rivers" or Tassili n'Ajjer national park, are some of the most important prehistoric drawings.

Unknown · *Kakadu Rock Paintings* · Australia ca. 50 BCE Kakadu National Park contains several sacred sites to the Aboriginal Australians, alive with dreamtime spirit. Kakada natives in partnership with the national government have successfully protected the culture and environment.

I believe artists find consternation and inspiration in open spaces. There might ultimately be walls, but you can imagine the space without them. You can imagine the inspired space without containing walls. The open spaces can possibly intimidate if not offered up with a delicate and confident hand. It is the people that roam these spaces creating limits or inspiring limitless time and space and inspiration. The keepers of the spaces, like Ballroom Marfa, can make or break the wheel of inspiration for artists. Open the widest wellspring of your mind; we will help make it happen here. That is how we make it work. It is the wide-open landscape, limitless light and stars, the gentle roll of time, the 18-wheelers full of cattle, and the proximity to Mexico, that make Marfa an inspiration to so many artists. A cup of coffee from Dairy Queen and a drive down to Pinto Canyon with no one else on the road gives you enough time to ponder what you are on the inside. It can help you to see what you stand for in the moment or in this lifetime. Marfa is a profound break from external bombardments and responses- the visual sound and your response to urban settings. For me, the immersive spaces in Mexico, the antique spaces, the pyramids, the altars, the neighborhoods of ancient times are the installations that inspire me. These are the artists and artisans that mystify and enliven me. If you are fortunate, we may encounter contemporary interventions by living artists in these antique spaces. Then you have really got something, right? The layers of time and intention revealing itself through the human hand. Land. Time. Human Intervention.

— **VIRGINIA LEBERMANN,** Co-founder of Ballroom Marfa, Marfa, Texas, 2024

(previous) Maximilien Bruggmann · *The Mystic Giraffes of Tagueït* · Switzerland · 2000 Just off the Trans-Siberian Highway in the Ténéré desert of the Air Mountains in Niger, Africa is the sandstone area of the largest petroglyphs in the world.

Unknown · *The Venus of Laussel or Woman with a Horn* · France · ca. 25,000 BCE Carved into the face of a rock, the Goddess figure found in 1911 in Laussel cave is located in the Dordogne valley of France. Differing interpretations agree she is the subject of magical or shamanistic purpose.

(previous) **Unknown**
*Petroglyphs at Newspaper
Rock, Utah* · **United
States** · 500–1500
Called "Tse' Hone" by
the Navajo, which
means "rock that tells
a story," is one of the
largest collection of
petroglyphs in the US.
Carved in both prehis-
toric and historic times,
the rock panel was
used as a wall of com-
munication, depicting
mythologies, seasonal
cycles, and hunting
strategies. Newspaper
Rock is one of many
petroglyph areas along
the sacred landscape
near Moab, Utah.

Unknown · *Three Rivers Petroglyph Site* · **United
States** · 900–1400 One of the largest petroglyph
sites in the southwest, Three Rivers is known for its
enormous collection of art. Geometric and abstract
in design, the art appears to tell a linear story specu-
lated to be similar to the Hopi origin story.

Unknown · *Bushmen (San) rock painting* · **South
Africa** · ca. 6000 BCE High up upon the rocky-
faced Drakensberg mountains, the San people left
behind thousands of rock paintings consisting of
horses, cattle, dogs, sheep, baboons, wild pigs,
elephants, snakes, birds, and humans.

(opposite)
Michael T. Bies
48FR31 Boulder
United States · 2013
Rock art from the
Dinwoody area of
Wyoming is one of the
greatest collections of
petroglyphs in the state,
where Native American
villages had a constant
supply of pure water,
wildlife, and fish all year
long. The petroglyphs
on these cliffs display
complex designs said
to be manifestations of
entities of the area.

Maximilien Bruggmann
Lady of Tagueït
Switzerland · 1992
Found at the Tagueït
rock art site in the des-
ert of the Air Mountains
in Niger, the female,
neolithic petroglyph lays
on the side of a dry riv-
erbed. The engravings
are thought to have
been created during the
Equidian period.

ELEMENT
Earth

ENERGY
Stillness
Silence

NOTE
D#

ALTARS OF THE ANCIENTS

Image in Nature
MOUNTAIN

COLOR
Blue · Green

MATERIALS
Stone

INTERCARDINAL DIRECTION
Northeast

Altars of the Ancients

O you temples fairer than lilies, pour'd over by the rising sun!
O you fables, spurning the known, eluding the hold of the known, mounting to heaven!
You lofty and dazzling towers, pinnacled, red as roses, burnish'd with gold!
Towers of fables immortal, fashion'd from mortal dreams!

— WALT WHITMAN, Poet & Seeker, from *A Passage to India*, 1871

Hard rock, curved, cut and hand-hewn, ancient wood, intricately etched with figures—the complex creation of sacred sites was manifested by our ancestors in a multitude of forms, from the circle of giant boulders erected at Stonehenge, to the mysterious sculpted heads of Easter Island, to the towering totem poles built by the indigenous peoples of the American Pacific Northwest.

The building of temples in veneration to gods and goddesses has been an integral part of our spiritual evolution—across cultures and around the globe. Over 2000 years ago, for instance, the Egyptians erected perhaps one of the most elaborate of these structures, the labyrinthine Temple of Karnak, which still stands today on the banks of the Nile River. Dedicated to the worship of the gods Amun, Mut, and Khonsu, the sprawling complex includes a vast array of sacred spaces, temples, and shrines. In Greece, the ancient culture left its enduring mark in the form of hundreds of temple ruins. One of the largest, The Parthenon, towers atop the Acropolis of Athens, and was contracted in the 5th century BCE in dedication to the goddess Athena.

In Cambodia, the five exquisitely carved stone towers at Angkor Wat were erected during the 12th century and are said to represent the sacred Mount Meru. Across the globe, on Mexico's Yucatan Peninsula, the ancient Mayan city of Chichen Itza was built over a period of several centuries, and includes a variety of buildings and structures, including the famous Temple of Kukulcan. With construction thought to have begun in the 6th Century, astronomical alignment and sacred geometry were key in the city's planning, as evidenced in The Caracol, a circular observatory, used to track the movements of the stars and in the Temple of Kukulan itself. The latter is a stepped pyramid with four sides, with each side containing 91 steps. Together, with the top of the platform, the Temple features a total of 365 steps, the number of days in the solar year. During the equinoxes at Kukulan, the sun's position casts a shadow on the pyramid, creating the illusion of a dark serpent descending the staircase. The desire to mark specific spaces as centers for veneration and worship, the need to erect monuments in dedication to the spiritual realm, this is an eternal and universal human longing.

(previous page) **Geremia Discanno** · *Plate 3 from Le case ed i monumenti di Pompei* · **Italy** · **1854** Discanno was commissioned to draw a recreation of the elaborately tiled "House of the Tragic Poet" in the ancient Roman city of Pompeii.

Unknown · *Totem poles in Stanley Park* · **Canada** ca. **1880** Exquisitely crafted totem pole artworks, created by various First Peoples artisans, are featured on display at a public park in Vancouver. The collection of nine totem poles were sourced from remote areas in British Columbia.

(opposite) Unknown
Atlantean figures
Mexico · ca. 750
Fifteen feet tall Toltec
statues hewn from a
single basalt rock, top
the Quetzalcólatl pyra-
mid in the Toltec city of
the sacred Tula valley.
With exceptional cosmic
knowledge, the city is
laid out in astronomical
design and appears to
have accommodated
large-scale ceremonial
rites.

Unknown · *Code of
Laws Stele of Hammurabi*
Iran · 1700 BCE
King Hammurabi of
Babylon shares the
scene with Shamash,
the sun God in the
photo of the basalt slab
of inscribed cuneiform
code. The text lays out
comprehensive laws for
a spectrum of offenses,
both criminal and civil.
The stele was found in
1901 in ancient Susa of
biblical notoriety.

There is a sense of freedom in Marfa, of open space, that makes it a conducive place to create art. When you think of the open space here in West Texas and that sense of freedom that comes with it, your mind tends to open as well. You are free from being inundated, by information, by buildings, by advertisements, by artificial lights, all those things one has to process when one lives in a populated space. Marfa, instead, has an expanse of desert and open skies and that natural environment offers a true meditative space for artists. It is a meditation to look out at the horizon, to gaze at all that vastness. The imagination comes in and fills that space and takes over. This is place that allows the imagination to expand. One of the first installations we did at the gallery was with the artist Agnes Denes, who brought the outside, in. She built four large pyramids, each representing an element. One was filled with Marfa tap water, another with recycled motor oil, one with water from the nearby Rio Grande, another was mirrored, and so reflected the viewer and the gallery around them. Another initiative we did was Marfa Sessions, *where there were immersive sound installations created all around the town. Another multimedia work,* Kite Symphony, *took its primary inspiration from being out in the Marfa landscape. Invited for a short visit, the artists, Roberto Carlos Lange and Kristi Sword, decided to prolong their stay in Marfa and ultimately created a film, an outdoor composition and installation, a series of drawings, sculpture, animation, performance and a soundtrack album. The result was a multidisciplinary collaboration directly inspired by Marfa itself. There is a feeling of smallness when you are in a place like Marfa. You're humbled by the nature here, the power of it. There are so many unknowns, and unexplored space, but in that smallness, you feel, there is a sense of both expansiveness and of peace.*

— FAIRFAX DORN, Curator, Gallerist,
& Co-Founder of Ballroom Marfa, 2024

Unknown · *Olmec Head* · Mexico · 1000–400 BCE A monolith head rests in the Tres Zapotes Mexican state of Veracruz. Carved from volcanic basalt, the colossal heads are thought to be warrior kings or rulers with spiritual or religious significance, and used in rituals, ceremonies, or significant events in the Olmec civilization.

Unknown · *Moai by the Quarry* · Easter Island 1400–1600 Painstakingly chiseled out of rock then mysteriously moved to their current locations, the iconic Maoi of Easter Island number over a thousand and each one is different.

Unknown · *View of the Treasury* · Jordan · 6th Century Carved out of sandstone, the spectacular facade was built to serve as a tomb for the Naba-taean King Aretas III. The lore of Petra's Treasury speaks of an Egyptian pharaoh who hid his trea-sure there as he pursued Moses and the Israelites.

Edgar Barclay · *Returning Home, Stonehenge, Wiltshire*
England · 1891 As a shepherd and his flock end
the day with a journey home, they pass by the great
prehistoric monument in the oil on canvas by
Barclay—an expert historian, writer, and speaker
on the history of Stonehenge.

Like meditation, ritual and other esoteric practices, a pilgrimage to a powerful sacred site is a way to access something outside of linear time and space. We are intuitively drawn to the energies, practices and places that can help us access past life attainments and deepen our understanding of our true nature. This isn't always a conscious process. Sometimes we are called to a site because there is a gift or element waiting there for us there that will be instrumental in activating higher levels of consciousness. Retrieving it can happen completely outside conscious awareness, and over time may reveal itself as a slow dawning of understanding, but also might be experienced as a flash of insight or a download of knowledge or power. If we have a strong enough of a relationship to a place, there might be several layers of energy that we are meant to access. If a site is powerful enough, it overwhelms and bypasses linear time and finite reality, and in that amplified space we can more easily access other realms and timelines. Prayers and rituals are more amplified, not only because the power of the place adds to and amplifies the power of the practitioner, but because the veils are thinner. Every sacred site has its own energetic signature. Certain practices are more powerful when there's a matching energy at a particular site. The Maratika Cave in Nepal, for instance, is one of the most powerful places on the planet to perform the Tibetan Buddhist Long Life Ritual. Many of the ancient churches and cathedrals were built on top of pagan sites of worship, and often the pagans themselves were practicing in places that, like in the case of Stonehenge, had been built thousands of years prior. For millennia there has been an understand that practicing on sacred sites and the portals, vortexes and leylines that they are often built upon, magnifies the power of the individual and their practice. When used with the best intentions, these sacred sites can help us access and unlock the greatest parts of ourselves.

— SANTOSH KHALSA, Scholar & Meditation Teacher, 2024

Frederic Sordeau · *Buddhist Monks in the inner part of Bayon Temple of Angkor Thom* · Cambodia · 2019
The temple, located at the center of the Angkor, was intended to represent Mt. Meru on earth, which is the center of the universe. Designed as a mandala, it reflects the cosmos. At the innermost area of the Bayon a central tower is surrounded by eight smaller towers, decorated with faces.

Unknown · *Izumo Taisha/Shimenawa Straw Rope* · Japan · 1744 Marking the entrance of the sacred Shinto shrine in Japan, hangs an enormous straw rope meant to keep impurity away. It measures forty-four feet long and weighs four tons. Izumo Taisha is said to be the place where all the gods meet every year in October.

Unknown · *Chichen Itza* · Mexico · 6th Century Called the Temple of Warriors, the astrologically designed pyramid and gathering place probably once held large crowds for ceremonial purposes including human sac-rifice, which held great importance in Mayan society. A large Chac Mool rests in the center of the summit, and one was found buried in an underground chamber.

Kees Scherer · *Relief in Edfu Temple* · Egypt 1968 The Edfu temple marks the site where the battle over the powers of good and evil between ancient Egyptian gods Horus and Set took place.

Constructed in the Ptolemaic dynasty, the temple is extensively decorated with reliefs of Gods, pharaohs, and inscriptions, as one of the most well-preserved Egyptian sacred sites.

ELEMENT
Earth

ENERGY
Movement
Growth

NOTE
$E^{\#}$

THE SEEDED SOIL

Image in Nature
THUNDER

COLOR
Green

MATERIALS
Soil

CARDINAL DIRECTION
East

The Seeded Soil

The best place to find God is in a garden. You can dig for him there.

— GEORGE BERNARD SHAW, Writer & Gardener, from a speech made in the early 1900s

The garden is a key symbol and centerpiece of spiritual mythologies throughout time and across belief systems. In many early traditions, gardens played an integral role in both origin and afterlife myths. Often depicted as realms created by the gods, gardens were seen as a place where humanity was both birthed and as a sanctuary we returned to in death, as reward for a life lived virtuously. For the ancient Greeks, the Elysian Fields were said to be paradise where souls would find rest in eternal happiness. Greek mythology also spoke of the Garden of the Hesperides, where nymphs stood guard over a tree bearing golden apples, which would bestow immortality if eaten. In Judeo-Christian tradition, the Garden of Eden was said to be where Adam and Eve lived in bliss before their expulsion by God. In Norse mythology, the Garden of the Gods, also known as Asgard, was depicted as a lush and verdant place, inhabited by a host of divine beings and deities.

The Hanging Gardens of Babylon, considered to be one of the Seven Wonders of the Ancient World, was believed to have been an immense garden complex built by King Nebuchadnezzar II for his wife—a place dedicated not only to the gods, but to love. The grand gardens of the Taj Mahal in India surround the iconic palace, a spread of luxuriant greenery and flowers inspired by spiritual concepts of paradise. In contrast, the minimalist raked stone gardens at Ryoan-ji Temple in Kyoto are perhaps the most famous Zen rock gardens in all of Japan.

The garden as mythical and meditative space, as a place of redemption and inspiration—is a symbolic component in a myriad of spiritual traditions. In Europe of the 11th century, the German abbess, mystic, artist and herbalist, Hildegard von Bingen tended to a renowned medicinal garden, her abbey not merely a religious sanctuary but place for healing—both spiritually and physically. Von Bingen chronicled her study of plant medicines in a nine-volume manuscript entitled, *Physica*. A visionary theologian, her prolific writings expressed radical views on nature as an embodiment of God, the garden, the green grass, the blooming flower, for her—all sacred, all sacraments. "Gaze at the beauty of earth's greenings," she famously wrote, "Now, think. What delight God gives to humankind with all these things. All nature is at the disposal of humankind."

(previous page) Unknown · *From The House of The Golden Bracelet* · Italy · 1st Century Named after the discovery of the remains of a woman wearing perfectly preserved jewelry, House of the Golden Bracelet is one of the most opulent in Pompeii.

Unknown · *The Unicorn Rests in a Garden* Netherlands · 1495–1505 One among 7 tapestries called "The Hunt of the Unicorn," filled with dense vegetation and symbolism, the fine wool and silk threads display 101 different varieties of plants, each with its own religious meaning.

MYSTICAL
ARCHITECTURE

Unknown · *Lady seated with mirror in a garden* India · 1909 Musicians play for a woman and her assistant in the Indian miniature painting. Known as a Bazaar painting, the style is defined by merging Western styles with traditional Indian imagery and depict a range of religious and secular subjects.

Jean Cotelle · *The Groves of Versailles: View of the Maze with Diana and her Nymphs* · France · 1688 The twenty-one paintings of The Gardens of Versailles depict every grove in the vast and manicured Versailles chateau grounds. The extensive design featured a Labyrinth, mythological fountains, and statues, all built along a north-south and east-west axis so the sun would rise and set in alignment to the home of King Louis XIV, by French landscape architect André Le Nôtre.

(opposite)
CiCi Suen · *The Garden Maze* · England · 2017 Capturing the secret world that can only be found in a garden, CiCi Suen's charcoal and pastel drawing gives the viewer an opportunity to enter a maze of mystery without context, in the children's book illustration.

Dorothy Eugénie Brett · *Umbrellas* England/United States 1917 A part of the collective of artists and writers known as the "Bloomsbury Set", Brett depicts her creative circle of Julien Morrell, Aldous Huxley, Brett herself, Ottoline Morrell, Lytton Strachey, John Middleton Murry, and Katherine Mansfield in the background.

Lucas Cranach the Elder · *The Golden Age* Germany · 1530 A celebratory dance set in a sacred garden, the artist envisions a utopian scene, perhaps dreaming of a world where we remain within the walled paradise of Eden.

Communities have long been a part of society as spiritual establish-
ments. However, an intentional community to me seems more organic.
It originates from a specific vision and seeks to meet the needs of the
individuals who either form it or are drawn to it. So, to me it has
a more dynamic charisma than say, a traditional community dating
back to Middle Ages that follows an abstract "Rule" and rigid rituals.
Members have more opportunity to participate in implementing the
community's vision and mission. Also, intentional communities
may include more diverse lifestyles and backgrounds than traditional religious communities which have accepted only renunciants as
candidates into its spiritual framework. The Ashram's origin was
unique. It originated from a Divine directive to the founder, Alice
Coltrane Swamini Turiyasangitananda, instead of someone's "great
idea." Based on the framework and practices, I viewed it as a spiritual vortex whose beautiful, natural setting of mountains, running
stream and sounds of nature offered a peaceful space for spiritual
seekers to pursue their practices, that urban life could never provide.
Our weekly worship services called kirtan were filled with conscious
intention and heartfelt worship. The service included a spontaneous
discourse from our spiritual teacher that concluded with her spir-
it-filled prayer for everyone present. The following worship of call
and response bhajan chanting included Sanskrit chants accompanied
by the teacher playing the organ. Percussion instruments enhanced the
chants. The philosophy taught was not Hinduism as many assume
which developed later from Vedanta. The core intent was to allow
serious aspirants to discover the true purpose of human life, God-
realization: to re-align with their divine god-Self, through cultivating
pure devotion for God.

— SHANKARI ADAMS
Educator and Meditation Practitioner & Author of
Portrait of Devotion: Spiritual Life of Alice Coltrane Swamini Turiyasangitananda

Hazel Florez · *Danu's
Garden* · United States
2022 Danu is the Celtic
Goddess of nature and
fertility. She is also
associated with fairies,
rivers, and lakes.
Painted in a supernatu-
ral spectrum of nature
and nature's beings in
coexistent harmony, her
domain thrives.

(following) Lodewijk
Toeput · *Pleasure
Garden with a Maze*
Belgium/Italy
1579–84 Known
for his formal gardens,
Toeput paints a maze
in a fantastical nature
scene with a Venetian
background and
a celebration of life's
pleasures.

Unknown · *Lavender Fiends of Abbey of Senanque* · France · 1148 Surrounded by a valley of lavender, the twelfth century Cistercian monastery is still in use by monks today, after a history of being destroyed during the religious wars.

(opposite, top) Unknown · *Holi Festival in a Walled Garden with Celebrants* · India · ca. 1764 The colorful Indian celebration of Holi marks the joyful passage of winter into spring and the triumph of good over evil.

(opposite, bottom) Gustav Klimt · *Flower Garden* Austria · 1907 Klimt choses a gentle and emotive garden scene in impressionism style in the third most expensive painting ever sold in Europe.

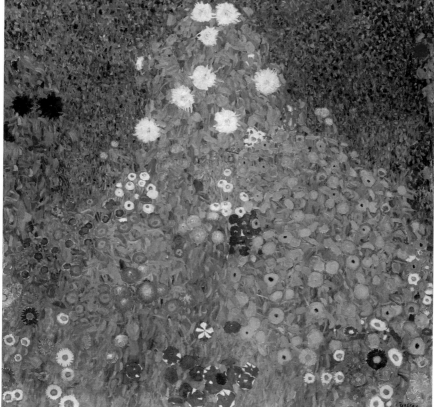

Lucian Freud
Garden, Notting Hill Gate · England · 1997
Renowned for its garden squares and private and community gardens, Notting Hill is the green scene in the painting by the grandson of Sigmund Freud, in a departure from his usual portrait paintings.

Edward James · *Las Pozas* · England · 1949–84
British poet Edward James materialized his surreal visions in the deep jungles of Mexico, constructing fantastical concrete structures of eccentric proportions. Resembling an ancient city lost to time, it hides in his 75-acre forest as a grand testament to his brilliance and commitment to build his own Garden of Eden.

═══
─ ─

NOTE
F$^{\#}$

SUBLIME ASCENSION

Image in Nature

WIND · AIR

COLOR
Purple · Blue

MATERIALS
Stone

INTERCARDINAL DIRECTION
Southeast

Sublime Ascension

The Great Pyramid was not a lighthouse, an observatory, or a tomb, but the first temple of the Mysteries.

— MANLY P. HALL, Philosopher & Scholar, from *The Secret Teachings of All Ages*, 1928

Rising to meet the very edges of the sky, the pyramid structure is ubiquitous on a global scale, sacred architecture among a wide range of cultures, often built as monuments to a higher power and as a center for a variety of religious, funerary, and spiritual ceremonies. Many pyramids were constructed specifically to align astronomically with the sun, moon, or stars, and were often built as tombs for deceased leaders, the pyramid itself is believed to provide a direct passage into the afterlife. Perhaps the most famous of these sites are the pyramids of Egypt, originally built as burial tombs, with the largest, The Great Pyramid of Giza, erected for the pharaoh Khufu. Construction on this vast temple complex began during the Old Kingdom period of ancient Egypt, around 2580 to 2560 BCE These ancient pyramids showcase feats of architectural engineering that remain impressive, even to the modern eye. Stones at Giza were exactly and expertly cut and many of the structures align precisely with the cardinal directions or key celestial movements or seasons of the year.

Many other ancient cultures, in far flung parts of the globe, also erected comparable pyramidical edifices. In India, the Mauryan Empire built similarly shaped mound temples

called, "stupas." These structures, such as the Great Stupa of Sanchi, served as Buddhist religious monuments. In ancient China, earthen pyramids were also built as burial mounds for emperors and nobility during the Shang, Zhou, and Han dynasties.

Meanwhile across the oceans, for the ancient Mesoamerican civilizations, the pyramid was also considered sacred, a place for ceremony and ritual. In Teotihuacan, Mexico, the Pyramid of the Sun and the Pyramid of the Moon, both built over 2,000 years ago were important sites of worship. Also in Mexico, the Pyramid of Kukulcan at Chichen Itza remains perhaps one of the most iconic of the Mayan-built pyramids, again featuring remarkably advanced architectural construction. Some researchers believe, in looking closely at the design and orientation of the Mesoamerican pyramids, that these structures were utilized not just for spiritual ceremony but for astronomical study and observation.

The pyramid shape itself is an example of sacred geometry and holds deep symbolic meaning, with each side converging to single point, which in many traditions is said to represent a connection between the earthly and divine realms.

(previous page) Unknown · *Akhnaten* · United States · 1984 The stylized poster for Phillip Glass' three-part opera features Akhnaten gracefully penetrating a pyramid into the sun. It is the story of the Egyptian Pharaoh who centered a whole religion around Aten, the Sun as God.

Unknown · *Pyramidion of Iufaa* · Egypt · 664–525 BCE Inscribed for Iufaa, a priest of Osiris, the ruler of the Netherworld, this steep-sided pyramidion was discovered the ancient site of Abydos and originally would have topped his sacred temple.

Unknown · *Arabs assisting tourists to climb the pyramids at Giza* · Egypt · ca. 1850 At one time, tourists could climb the great pyramid. Egyptians stationed along the way helped boost them up the limestone rocks for all 451 feet to the top. As a preservation effort, it is now illegal to climb the pyramids.

Hubert Robert · *Alexander the Great visiting the Tomb of Achilles* · France · 1760 The artist imagines the supposed Troy burial ground, where Achilles died, rumored to be a ritual site visited by many famed historical figures.

Ahmed Karaly
*A Pyramid in Other
Vocabularies* · Egypt
2022 Ahmed Karaly's
sculpture is a modern,
lit pyramid, in the
multi-artist installation
"Forever is Now," on
the sands of the Giza
plateau. With a mod-
ern-day perspective of
constructing a pyramid,
he aimed to erect
a geometric structure
with a contemporary
understanding of
the principles behind
the shape.

Unknown · *The Great
Sphinx and the Pyramids
of Giza* · Egypt · 1924
Manly P. Hall wrote of
his exploration of the
pyramids, 'The Great
Pyramid was not a light-
house, an observatory,
or a tomb, but the first
temple of the Myster-
ies, the first structure
erected as a repository
for those secret truths
which are the certain
foundation of all arts
and sciences.'

Unknown · *Pyramid of Meidum* · Egypt · 3rd
Century BCE Originally a seven-tiered structure,
the Meidum Pyramid is thought to have been initially
built by Huni, the last pharaoh of the 3rd Dynasty,
and finished by his son Sneferu. It was the first
straight-sided pyramid in Egypt.

I have a deep connection with the Ancient Holy Lands of Kemet, also known as Egypt. This land has been a significant part of my path for a long time. I regularly go on pilgrimages there and host initiation journeys for those who feel the call. These lands resonate with me deeply because of the depth of the sacred architecture, the life-giving Holy Waters of the Nile, the celestial mappings that replicate heavenly realms on earth, and the ancient ritual practices of offerings that attend to all interdependent relations. Among these wonders is the only known eight-sided pyramid, the Great Pyramid. It's part of the only remaining ancient wonder of the world and aligns with sacred sites globally. Then there's the Sphinx, shrouded in mystery regarding its true age. Together, these structures are part of a grand network of pyramids and temples, both above and below ground. They are synchronized with certain star systems, forming what is known to be a Golden Mean map of relations. The mysteries of these Sacred Sites continually unfold, revealing deeper parts of ourselves, our origins, and who we truly are. Given that there is still so much being uncovered in these lands, and in sacred sites all over the world, we will never stop learning. The more we learn about these sites, the more we remember deeper parts of ourselves, our origins, and who we really are. Engaging with these mysteries, whether in physical form or through study, awakens deeper interior faculties and intelligences. This awakening enables us to create a legacy of beauty and belonging. It serves the web of life for future generations, helping us remember deeper parts of ourselves and our origins.

— ISIS INDRIYA, Scholar & Founder Academy of Oracle Arts, 2024

(following pages)
Manzel Bowman
End Game · United States · 2016 Merging Afrofuturism with collage art and science fiction, Bowman's pharaonic psychedelia vibrantly alter misrepresentations of black culture. His digital landscapes and figures transcend the normative American narrative.

Hilma af Klint · *Altarpiece - No. 1* · Sweden · 1915 One of a group of three paintings known as *Paintings for the Temple*, the iconic art correlates to the Theosophical spiritual philosophy of evolution as ascension from above to below and vice versa— the pyramid being the pinnacle of mystic knowledge and realized beingness.

(opposite)
John Augustus Knapp
Pythagoras
United States · 1926
Pythagoras holds a three-dimensional pyramid to demonstrate his famous theorem. He believed in a relationship between numbers and geometrical forms and thought the entire cosmos was constructed out of right triangles.

(top) Unknown · *Kukulcan's Pyramid at Chichen Itza* Mexico · 8th Century A few of El Castillo, also known as Kukulcan's Pyramid, built in the 8th century and one of the most iconic examples of Mesoamerican spiritual architecture.

I. M. Pei · *Louvre Pyramid* · France · 1989 Giving a nod to the sacred architecture of the ancients, the contemporary designer Yeoh Ming Pei created a new entrance to the iconic Louvre with his Pyramide in the Cour Napoleon.

J.A.KNAPP. 26

ELEMENT
Fire

ENERGY
Radiance

NOTE
G#

TEMPLES OF THE EAST

Image in Nature
FIRE · GLOW

COLOR
Red

MATERIALS
Wood · Stone

CARDINAL DIRECTION
South

Hindu & Buddhist Temples

I bite a persimmon
The bells toll—
Horyu-Ji Temple.

— SHIKI MASAOKA, Poet & Author, 1892

The temples and shrines of Hindu, Buddhist and other religious practices of the East are marked by the same striving and seeking of the sacred architecture of the West— carved stone and etched wood standing for centuries as centers for worship and spiritual teaching.

The Angkor Wat temple complex in Cambodia, built in the 12th century, is the Hindu temple considered to be one of the largest religious monuments in the world. The Golden Temple, also known as Harmandir Sahib, located in Amritsar, India is a sacred place of worship for Sikhs, built in the 16th century. In China, the Temple of Heaven, built in the early 15th century, is thought to have played a significant role in imperial ceremonies during the Ming and Qing dynasties. In Myanmar, the Shwedagon Pagoda is believed to contain relics of the Buddha and has been attracting pilgrims for centuries. The central stupa here is covered in gold and is said to be imbedded with thousands of diamonds and other precious stones.

In Japan, the Itsukushima Shrine, located on the island of Miyajima, features a distinctive torii gate, which appears to float when the tides are high. Torii gates are found at the entrance of many Shinto shrines and feature two vertical columns with a horizontal beam on top, a doorway of sorts, meant to symbolize the transition from the secular world into the sacred space within. The ornate Meiji Shrine in Tokyo was built in 1920 and dedicated to Emperor Meiji and his wife, Empress Shoken, is located on a large swath of forested land within the city and features traditional Japanese architecture and exquisitely planted gardens. In the city of Kyoto, the Zen temple of Tōfuku-ji is also known for its beautifully serene gardens. Also in Kyoto, Daitokuji is one of the largest of Japan's temple complexes and is considered to be the country's most prominent center for Zen practice.

Whether worshipping within luxuriantly adorned halls of gold or praying meditatively in raked rock or ritualistically-planted gardens, sacred spaces remain united by intention— sites built to enhance humanity's enduring connection, not only to spirit, but to ourselves.

(previous page) Unknown · *Swayambhunath* · Nepal 6th Century The great stupa of dharmakaya at the temple palace in the Kathmandu Valley also called Monkey Temple, is an important Buddhist pilgrimage site.

Alice S. Kandell · *Lamas play horns at temple door, Sikkim* · United States · ca. 1970 Monks are photographed here playing the gyaling, a traditional woodwind instrument mainly in Tibetan monasteries and is associated with peaceful deities and the idea of devotion.

ब्रह्मासन ७४

(opposite)
Hasui Kawase · *Spring Evening at Toshogu Shrine in Ueno* · Japan 1948 The holy place dedicated to the samurai leader Tokugawa Ieyasu, the most famous warrior in Japan, is a place of worship for the Shinto religion. Painter and printmaker Kawase portrays its five-storied pagoda.

Unknown · *Yogi from Asanas and Mudras* India · 19th Century A nineteenth century hatha yoga manual describes the different bodily postures and hand gestures done to concentrate energy for health and spiritual evolution. The yogi practices on the steps of a temple peak.

(previous) Unknown · *Paro Taktsang* · Bhutan 1692 Known as "Tiger's Nest," the high, cliffside Taktsang Monastery in Bhutan is the holy meditation site where Padmasambhava, or Guru Rinpoche, gave his famous Vajrayana teachings, and most importantly, where he taught Yeshe Tsogyal.

Gyula Tornai · *At the Shrine* · Hungary · 1907 A classically costumed Japanese woman gives supplications to the enshrined deity in an ornate temple. Gyula Tornai was an internationally known painter of far eastern scenes.

Unknown · *Suan Pakkad Palace, Lacquer Pavilion* Thailand · 17th Century What is now a museum was first a part of a palace built in Ayudhya, the birthplace of Thailand. It moved two times before ending up in its current location and being restored to its original glory with gold and black lacquer murals depicting the life of Buddha and the Indian epic, Ramayana.

Unknown · *Buddhist Mani Stone* · India · Date Unknown 'Om mani padme hum' is painted with a carving of Padmasambhava on a stone in Northern India. The mantra is a Tibetan Buddhist prayer associated with the bodhisattva, Avalokiteshvara. Rocks painted with the mantra line paths and walls leading to temples or stupas.

(following) Kenro Izu *Angkor #158. Cambodia (Temple of Ta Prohm)* Japan · 1996 With crumbling walls being swallowed up by giant, hundred-year-old tree roots, the once intricately designed temple dedicated to the mother of Buddhist king Jayavarman VII has become a dilapidated shell, as is detailed in the platinum print shot.

Unknown · *Mural from the Silver Pagoda* · Cambodia 1903–04 The Silver Pagoda in Phnom Penh is enclosed by walls plastered with an enormous fresco depicting the classic Indian epic of the Ramayana (known as the Reamker in Cambodia). The mural includes the famed Battle of Lanka.

Unknown · *Confucius Presenting the Young Gautama Buddha to Lao Tzu* · China · 19th Century San jiao, or the three teachings, refers to Confucianism, Taoism and Buddhism all coexisting in harmony, and is symbolized by the founding teachers representing their religions in the sixth century painting.

Unknown · *Indra Sabha in Cave XXXII* · India 9th Century Situated in Ellora India, a cave with the God Indra, seated on his elephant Airavata, is carved out of rock off of a basalt cliff. It is part of an extensive and monumental cliff-built series of caves, temples, and monasteries over a mile long, captured in this photograph circa 1874.

Unknown · *Kailasa Cave Temple at Ellora* India · 8th Century Constructed as a dedication to Lord Shiva, the remarkably-carved temple was commissioned by the queen of Elapura after petitioning Lord Shiva to heal the incurable illness of her husband, the king. He gradually improved and the queen quickly set out to build the temple to honor the Lord.

(opposite) Unknown *Sri Venkataramana Swamy Hindu Temple* · India 1689 India is home to a group of intricately designed temples. Famous for their erotic sculptures, Indian art, architecture, and symbolism, each is named after a particular God.

NOTE
A[#]

HOUSES OF WORSHIP

Image in Nature
GROUND · EARTH

Churches, Mosques & Synagogues

The central ideas for creating a sacred space have to do with truth and authenticity, a search for clarity, peace, transparency, a yearning for tranquility, a place to evoke other worldliness in a way that is uplifting. And to express spirituality, the architect has to think of the original material of architecture, of space and light.

— RICHARD MEIER, Architect & Artist—from an interview, 2014

Built in homage to one's chosen god, from the arched stone cathedral to the intricately tiled mosque, to the ancient synagogue, the stunning architecture of the world's predominate modern religions serve as sites of both worship and elation for millions of individuals across the globe.

The Great Mosque of Mecca, also known as the Kaaba, is one of the most important and sacred mosques in the world. Located in Saudi Arabia, it is the holiest site of Islam, and every year, millions of Muslims make a pilgrimage to the mosque for the Hajj. Another famous mosque is the Blue Mosque, also known as the Sultan Ahmed Mosque, in Istanbul, Turkey. This mosque, built in the early 17th century, is known for its unique six minarets and intricate blue tilework. The Sheikh Zayed Grand Mosque in Abu Dhabi is also an important mosque known for its modern Islamic architecture and pristine white marble exterior.

In Rome's Vatican City, the sprawling interior of St. Peter's Basilica, the largest Catholic church in the world, can hold up to 60,000 devout. On the ceiling of its

Sistine Chapel, Adam reaches out, eternally seeking the hand of God in Michelangelo's renowned mural. In France, the Notre-Dame de Paris, built in the 12th century, is hailed as a marvel of Gothic architecture. In Spain, the visionary architect Gaudi began the construction of the Sagrada Familia church in 1882, with its evolution still ongoing today. A masterpiece of Catalan Modernism, the church is known for its unique designs, combining Gothic and Art Nouveau elements to create a one-of-a-kind architectural marvel.

In Judaism, the Western Wall, also known as the Wailing Wall, is one of the most famous synagogues in the world. Located in the Old City of Jerusalem, it is the holiest site in Judaism. The Hurva Synagogue, located in Jerusalem's Jewish Quarter, is also a landmark synagogue, known for its dome-shaped skylight and intricate interior decoration.

With their immense scale, intricate workmanship, and ongoing evolutions, these religious sites are not only sacred but deeply inspiring to people of all faiths—spaces where artistry and architecture, creativity, and worship—unite and coalesce.

(previous page) Dmitri Kessel · *The painter Henri Matisse in the Chapel of the Rosary* · Ukraine/United States · 1951 Built and decorated between 1947 and 1951 by the artist Henri Matisse, the Chapelle du Rosaire de Vence, a small Catholic chapel located in the town of Vence on the French Riviera.

Mohammadreza Domiriganji · *Shah Imam Mosque* United Arab Emirates · 2014 A marvel of Islamic architecture, the dome of the Shah Mosque in Isfahan, Iran is designed in exquisite mosaics, masterfully laid in patterns of complex composition, and is considered a masterpiece.

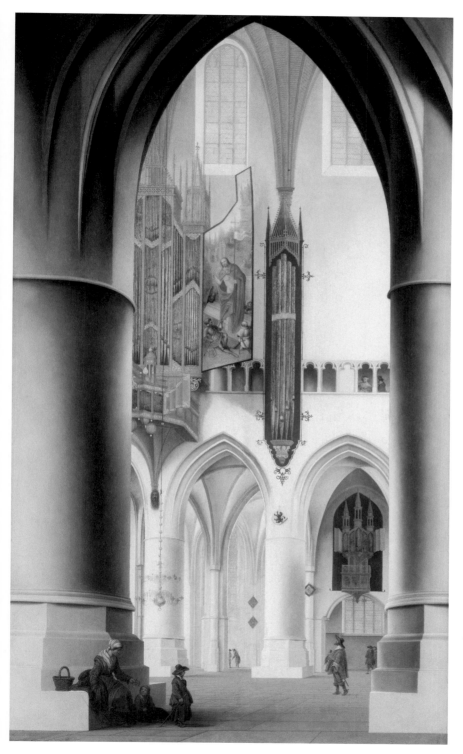

(opposite) France
Depré · *Interior of the
Grand Synagogue of
Edirne* · France · 1901
Edirne, Turkey is a city
known for its mosques
and Islamic-Ottoman
churches and bazaars
and the birthplace of
religious freedom for
Jews in the Ottoman
period when the Edirne
synagogue was built.
When the Jewish con-
gregation left the area,
it was abandoned and
went into disrepair. In
2015 it was restored
by the Turkish Founda-
tions Institute.

Pieter Jansz Saenredam
*Interior of the Church
of St Bavo in Haarlem*
Netherlands · 1636
Gothic St Bavo's in
Haarlem is the church z
seems to have depicted
most often, producing at
least twelve different artworks of the cathedral's
interior between 1628
and 1660.

Unknown
*Donati's Comet over
Notre-Dame* · France
1877 Discovered by
Italian astronomer
Giovanni Battista
Donati, the comet was
the brightest and closest
one to ever be seen and
photographed on earth.
The illustration was
published in 'Le Ciel'
(The Sky) by French
author Amedee
Guillemin, showing
the comet's flight over
Notre Dame.

(opposite)
Jerry de Wilde · *Spiral
Stairwell / Nativity
Tower / La Sagrada
Familia* · United States
1969 Built with the
intention to be a uni-
versal masterpiece of
Christian symbolism,
the epic Passion Tower
facade boldly hovers
above the giant basilica
of intricate geometric
and kaleidoscopic
design by Antonio
Gaudí. The winding
staircase in Gaudi's last
architectural feat
and is based on the
Fibonacci sequence.

Pascal Lemaitre
Our Lady of All Grace
France · 2013
The church of Notre-
Dame de Toute Grâce
in Plateau d'Assy in
France designed by
Maurice Novarina was
became the subject of
disapproval due to the
commissioning of art by
well known, yet secular
artists such as
Pierre Bonnard, Marc
Chagall, Ferdinand
Léger, Jacques Lipchitz,
Jean Lurçat, and
Henri Matisse.

Kenny Scharf and Okuda San Miguel *International Church of Cannabis interior* United States · 2017 Known as Elevationists, the congregation of the cannabis church in Denver use "the sacred flower" to achieve higher states of consciousness for self-mastery. Famed NYC artist Kenny Scharf and Spanish muralist Okuda San Miguel wowed the walls and ceilings with rainbowed amazement.

(following pages) Andrea Pozzo · *Entry of St Ignatius into Paradise* Italy · 1685–94 The intricate fresco details St Ignatius of Loyola, the Spanish knight and theologian who founded the Society of Jesus.

(opposite, top) Muhammad Salih · *Ceiling at Abdulaziz Khan Madrassah* · Uzbekistan · 1652 Architectural monument, The Abdulaziz Khan Madrasah, with its rich colored Islamic patterns and gilded ornaments was built in 1652 by the Khan of Bukhara in Uzbekistan.

(opposite, bottom) Mohammad Hasan-e-Memār and Mohammad Rezā Kāshi-Sāz-e-Širāzi · *Nasir al Molk Mosque* · Iran · 1888 The majestically patterned mosque in Shiraz, Iran, known as the Pink Mosque or Rainbow Mosque becomes a kaleidoscope when the sun hits the stained-glass windows.

James T. Hubbell
Sea Ranch Chapel
United States · 1985
Sea Ranch, California
residents Robert and
Betty Buffem built the
architectural treasure as
a nondenominational
sanctuary for meditation
and prayer. Designed
by James T. Hubbell,
it aligns with his philosophy to create unique
living environments in
harmony with nature.

Unknown · *The Church
of Saint George* · Ethiopia
13th Century
Called Bete Giyorgis
in Ethiopia, the King
Lalibela built the below
ground, rock hewn
church to venerate one
of Christianity's most
celebrated warrior saints.

(opposite, top) Manly
P. Hall · *Pearl Mosque –
Moti Masjid (Agra Fort)*
United States · 1924
Made entirely of white
marble, the 17th cen-
tury mosque was built
by Mughal Emperor
Shah Jahan.

(opposite, bottom)
Lloyd Wright
Wayfarers Chapel
United States · 1951
Built by Lloyd Wright,
son of Frank Lloyd
Wright, the chapel was
created as a dedication
to Emanuel Swedenborg,
scientist, and theologian.

(following, left) Sander Berg · *The Church Grim* Sweden · 2020 The Scandinavian church grim is a folkloric creature, buried in the foundation of a church prior to construction, thought to forever protect and guard the grounds, illustrated in its spirit form by Berg.

(following, right) Unknown · *Gol Stave Church* · Norway · 1884 Elaborately carved from timber, this reconstructed stave church in Norway is adorned with dragon heads, foliage, and snakes. A runic inscription at the entrance attests to the pagan beliefs that merged with the Norse and Christian ideology of the Vikings who built it.

(pages 314–315) Ludwig Förster *Torah Ark of the Great Synagogue on Dohany Street* · Hungary 1859 The architect of the synagogue designed it based on the opinion of an absence of a definitive Jewish style. The final design took on an Islamic, North African, and Medieval Spanish decor.

NOTE
B#

SPACES OF REFLECTION

Image in Nature
LAKE · MARSH

Monasteries & Meditation Centers

The less there was of me, the happier I got.

— LEONARD COHEN, Poet, Musician, & Meditator, circa 1980s

(previous page)
Carl Gustav Carus
Gothic Windows in the
Ruins of the Monastery
at Oybin · **Germany**
ca. 1828 Sitting atop the
mountains of Zittau in
Germany, rest the ruins
of Oybin. Once a mon-
astery for the Order of
the Celestines, it fell to
ruin during reformation,
leaving the abandoned
edifice to succumb to
nature, inspiring painters
like Carus. The beauty
of the remains has
attracted and inspired
many works from multi-
tudes of artists.

Constructed for retreat, for respite, as a space to sit in silence and isolation in order to better hear the teachings of god or spirit—monasteries and meditation centers exist around the globe, each showcasing a wide variety of religious dogmas and practices. The Shaolin Monastery in China for instance, founded in the 5th Century, is known for its association with Zen Buddhism and the instruction in martial arts, the site considered to be the birthplace of Kung Fu. In Thailand, the Wat Phra Dhammakaya Temple is a well-known med- itation center which houses a giant golden statue of Buddha. The Phugtal Monastery, perched high on a cliff in the remote regions of Zanskar Valley, in India, is one of the most isolated monasteries in the world, famous for its vibrant and intricately deco- rated prayer halls.

In France, on the island of Mont Saint- Michel, just off the Normandy coast, sits the Roman Catholic monastery and abbey of the same name, dating back to the 8th century. Skellig Michael, also located on a remote island, off the coast of Ireland, is known for its ancient monastic settlement with hermitages on the island dating as far back as the 6th century.

Among the many renowned contemporary meditation centers in the world is Plum Village, founded by Thich Nhat Hanh, the Vietnamese Buddhist monk and peace activist. Located in France, Plum Village, founded in 1982, has hosted thousands of meditators each year with a core mission of cultivating peace, compassion, and mindfulness in both individuals and society. The Vipassana International Meditation Center, based in India, is one of the most well-known medi- tation centers in the world, its technique and teachings rooted in the Buddhist principles of insight and awareness. In North America, the Insight Meditation Society is one of the leading meditation centers in the West, with outposts in various locations offering silent meditation retreats and classes based on Theravada Buddhist teachings.

As a space for those seeking either solitary and monastic study or guided meditative paths to enlightenment, the architecture of these sites almost always aligns itself with both contemplation and community. As with the Tarot arcana of The Hermit, one may take the lonesome path to the spiritual summit, but eventually one must return from the mountain top to share knowledge and insights gained and to light the path ahead for others.

Unknown · *The Jewel of the Essence of All Sciences*
India · 1840 The image is taken from the European, Islamic, and Indian traditions astrological manuscript written by Durgāshankara Pāthaka, a well-known astronomer from Benares. Guru Nanak is pictured, to whom teachings of Sikhism are attributed.

PART III

Unknown · *Life of
Padmasambhava (detail)*
Tibet · 18th Century
Scenes from the life
of Padmasambhava
are the subject of the
painting which also
pictures Tibetan King
Trisong Detsen and
abbot Santarakshita
who built Samyé, the
first Buddhist monastery
in Tibet—shaped
like a mandala.

Unknown · *Guru Nanak
with Friends* · India
16th Century Founder
and guru of Sikhism,
Nanak sits with his
companion Bhai Bala,
engaged in kirtan,
or devotional signing
of sacred mantra
or scriptures.

Vincenzo Abbati
*View of the Courtyard of
a Monastery* · Italy
19th Century
The elegant rendering
of monks and a nun
with the walls of a mon-
astery with a statue of a
saint in the foreground
reveals the inner sanc-
tum of monastic
life. Abbati was known
for depictions of places
of worship.

(opposite)
Paramahansa Yogananda
*The Lake Shrine at the
Self Realization Fellowship*
United States · 1950
Yogananda envisioned
a spiritual center where
people from all over
could come to experi-
ence peace of heart and
mind. The California
Lake Shrine offers a
Meditation Garden with
shrines and waterfalls,
a hilltop Temple with
spiritual services and an
ashram for monks.

*My work is an honoring of the sacred. The sacred earth, the sacred
feminine divine, and an honoring of the female body as sacred. I create
immersive installations that are sacred spaces, or temples, and activate
these spaces with communal engagement—sound healings, medita-
tions, performances. My sculptures are intended to harness energy and
are made from metal, an organic, earthly material. The drawings /
paintings function as both a representation of the female form and as
a spiritual diagram, with the intention to invite the viewer into a meditative state. The films are shot at sacred sites, and I am using sculptures as sacred objects to reflect the light of the Sun—cosmic energy. My
body is touching the earth and acting as a bridge between the earthen
and the cosmic. Through communal engagement I activate sacred space
within my work. My works are spiritual tools that have a use-value.
They are not static commodities. They are sacred objects meant to be
engaged with on some level. Sacred sites activate my creativity the most.
They activate my DNA! Ancient sites, pre-patriarchal, matrifocal sites
are my favorites. They connect with a Divine Feminine energy that is
palpable, and transportive. This is where I feel most alive. My work
is basically bringing this energy into an exhibition space. I think of
my exhibitions as interventions where I am inserting divine feminine
consciousness into commercial or institutional spaces. The Phoenician
Tombs in Ibiza have a special resonance for me. They are located across
the sea from Es Vedra, another sacred site that features prominently
in my films. In ancient times the Phoenicians would pilgrimage to the
small isle to leave offerings to the Goddess Tanit. Tanit is my patron
Goddess, and when I am performing within Her sacred sites, I am
calling on Her to enter me, and to use my body as a vessel. These
ancient sacred sites speak to the worship of a female deity, this is why
they resonate so deeply with me. They are vestiges of a Truth that has
been suppressed for millennia, and my purpose is to reintegrate this
Truth into contemporary culture.*

— KATHRYN GARCIA, Artist, 2024

**Luigi Busi · *Meditation*
Italy · 19th Century**
A nun sits in open-eyed
reflection, gazing sky-
ward in her apparent
practice. Meditation for
the nun or monk is a
deconstruction of mental
agitation, to quell the
drives and desires of the
normal human condi-
tion. The oil on canvas
conveys the lonely jour-
ney of such.

≡

NOTE
C#

HONORING THE DEAD

Image in Nature
HEAVEN · SKY

COLOR
Gray

MATERIALS
Soil · Stone

INTERCARDINAL DIRECTION
Northwest

Cemeteries & Monuments

Old Yew, which graspest at the stones
That name the under-lying dead,
Thy fibres net the dreamless head,
Thy roots are wrapt about the bones.

— LORD ALFRED TENNYSON, Poet, from *In Memoriam*, 1850

Nearly all sacred sites are associated with the afterlife and death—whether it be the monuments to the great pharaohs or ancient temples odes to underworld deities or sprawling gothic cathedrals—each contains space for memorializing those loved and lost. Cemeteries and monuments have long been places to honor, remember, and pay respects to those who have passed. Graveyards and cemeteries often sit side by side to the churches and holy sites where the living still flock to worship.

Some of the most famous monuments to the dead include the elaborate mausoleum at the Taj Mahal in India, built by Emperor Shah Jahan in memory of his wife, who passed away during childbirth. In the United States, at the Arlington National Cemetery, more than 400,000 soldiers are buried, including those who fought in the Civil War, World War I, World War II, and other conflicts. Egypt's ancient Valley of the Kings is the burial ground for many famous pharaohs, including Tutankhamun and Ramses II. Mount Koya Cemetery in Japan holds immense spiritual significance in Buddhism as the burial place of the renowned Buddhist monk Kukai. The Père Lachaise Cemetery in Paris, France is known for its hauntingly beautiful architecture and as the final resting place of many famous personalities including, Jim Morrison, Oscar Wilde, and Frédéric Chopin. In London England, Highgate Cemetery features equally moody Gothic architecture and Victorian-era graves. Notable figures buried here include Karl Marx and George Eliot.

In many cultures, the dead are remembered, even long after burial, in vibrant annual rites and holidays, celebrations such as Day of the Dead and the pagan sabbath of Samhain. The Day of the Dead, or Dia de los Muertos, is a traditional Mexican rite which originated from indigenous Mesoamerican cultures, particularly the Aztec civilization. It is celebrated on November 1st and 2nd each year, aligning with the Catholic holidays of All Saints' Day and All Souls' Day. The festival has its roots in the belief that during these days, the spirits of the deceased come back to visit their loved ones. It is seen as a time to honor and remember the departed and celebrate the continuing cycle of life and death.

(previous page) Lei Yixin · *Stone of Hope* · China 2011 In Washington DC's national memorial park stands the Martin Luther King Jr. statue, the first African American to be memorialized in this way. The civil rights leader was carved from granite by Lei Yixin.

Shah Jahan · *The Taj Mahal* · India · 1648
The Taj-Mahal in India mirrors its perfect symmetry in a reflection pool. It was commissioned by the emperor Shah Jahan as a mausoleum for his wife, Mumtaz Mahal. It has become a symbol of the rich heritage of the Indian Empire.

(previous pages)
Unknown · *Mausoleums*
Iran · 11th Century
Domed, octagonal
crypts, as symbols of
heaven and eternal
life, in Turkish design
with indestructible
interiors, sit amongst
the mountains in Iran.
The exteriors are in
varying states of repair
due to earthquake
damage, yet still
they've stood since
the eleventh century.

Jerry de Wilde · *"Calvari"/Turó de les tres creus -
Park Güell* · United States · 1969 Barcelona's Park
Güell is one of Antoni Gaudi's artful masterpieces
that included his place of residence. The three
crosses atop the stone structure on the hill are called
the Turo de las Tres Creus.

Skidmore, Owings & Merrill (David M. Childs)
One World Trade Center · United States · 2014 The
tallest building in the United State, Freedom Tower
was built after the destroyed original twin towers
during the September 11th attack. The skyscraper
stands as a symbol of rebirth and resilience.

(following pages)
Christopher Mark
Perez · *Père Lachaise
Cemetery* · France
2018 Resting place of
Jim Morrison, Edith Piaf,
and Oscar Wilde, the
Paris celebrity cemetery
draws the most visitors
of any necropolis in the
world. A stroll through
the vast grounds is
a journey through
France's history and
heritage.

Unknown · *Buddha Statue* · China · 8th Century
Hewn from the side of Mount Emai in Leshan,
China, is the largest Buddha statue in the world.
It was carved in the first century along with many
temples within an impressive landscape of rich
and beautiful vegetation.

Gerson Fehrenbach · *The Münchener Strasse Synagogue
Monument* · Germany · 1963 On the "Night of
Broken Glass" a Nazi-instigated attack on Jews
destroyed hundreds of synagogues. The memorial
statue, erected in 1963, stands on the former site of
a synagogue in Berlin's Schöneberg district.

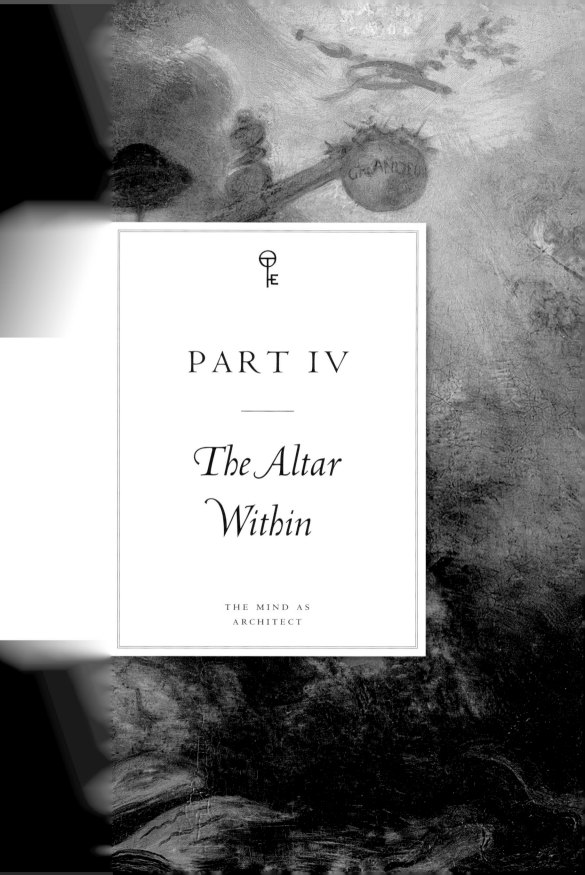

PART IV

—

The Altar Within

THE MIND AS
ARCHITECT

IMAGINED WORLDS

Exploring the Lands of Myth

In Xanadu did Kubla Khan
A stately pleasure-dome decree:
Where Alph, the sacred river, ran
Through caverns measureless to man
Down to a sunless sea.

— SAMUEL TAYLOR COLERIDGE, Poet & Seeker,
from the poem *Kubla Khan: or A Vision in a Dream*, 1816

Alice enters the cosmic portal of the rabbit hole, falling through multiple dimensions of time and space to emerge into Wonderland— the realm of the psychedelic, the subconscious, a dazzling dreamscape. Dorothy is swept from the eye of the tornado into the alternate universe of Oz and begins her surrealist adventure down the road of yellow brick. A young and unassuming hobbit opens his front door and travels far from his tiny village, on a grand and heroic quest through Middle Earth.

Spaces are made sacred by the battles fought there and in the archetypes of heroes inhabited, in the quests taken and the kingdoms gained. In Arthurian legend, the island of Avalon is linked to the magical sword Excalibur and the mystical Lady of the Lake. In the lost land of Atlantis, which some believe sunk tragically into the ocean's depths, there is said to have once lived a great and advanced civilization. El Dorado is another forgotten empire, rumored to have been rich beyond dreams in gold and treasure, a place sought in vain by Spanish conquistadors on their arrival in South America.

Sites are made sacred by their universality, by our shared and enduring conceptions—the idea of heaven and hell, for instance, of the worlds of fantasy and nightmare that linger just at the edges of our own. The pleasure and rewards of the afterlife takes on a multitude of forms and interpretations—depending on era, tradition, religion, or mythology. In Christian theology, heaven is typically understood as the eternal dwelling place of God and the blessed destination of those who have lived a righteous life. In Hinduism, heaven is known as Swarga or Svarga Loka, one of the many planes of existence in the cycles of death and rebirth. For the ancient Egyptians, heaven was associated with the concept of the Field of Reeds, a paradise-like place of abundance, where the deceased could enjoy eternal bliss.

(previous pages) Jean-Honoré Fragonard · *The Dream of Plutarch* · France · 18th Century A most prolific French artist, Fragonard portrays Greek philosopher Plutarch in a meditative repose.

Ivan Bilibin · *The Tale of Tsar Saltan* · Russia · 1831 Adapted into many variations and languages, the scene from the folk tale is an illustration of the mythical island of Buyan where the mother and son land after being tossed to sea in a sealed barrel.

И. БИЛИБИНЪ. 1905.

In literature and folk tales, reality is constantly in vivid flux, domains birthed by the creator's own imagination, rich and ripe with details, cultures, creatures, fauna, and flora that exist only within the storyteller's (and subsequently the reader's) mind. In J.R.R. Tolkien's world of novels, his Middle-Earth is populated not only by hero hobbits, but by wizards, orcs, elves, and dwarves, all who wander through a strange, stunning landscape, from the Misty Mountains to the forests of Lothlórien. The magical academy of Hogwarts in J.K. Rowling's creations is another enchanted place, a school where young magicians study alongside dragons and unicorns. In C.S. Lewis' chronicles, the land of Narnia is accessed by a mysterious wardrobe, allowing children to escape the perils of wartime England and into a world of talking animals and mythical creatures. Yet even in Narnia, there is an ongoing battle, a mythic fight of good against evil. George R.R. Martin's Westeros, Ursula K. Le Guin's Earthsea, the many multifaceted futurist landscapes of the writer Jules Verne—each creates their own vibrant and unique worlds—sacred to all those who venture forth between their pages. The imagined landscapes of fiction and myth, of folk tale and song, all poignantly resonate in our shared consciousness—our journeys into the unknown guided by the mystical visions of poets, artists, mythologists, and storytellers.

Rockwell Kent · *Richard Wagner, Das Rheingold, The Entrance of the Gods into Valhalla* · United States 1929 American artist reimagines the Norse concept of the afterlife, depicting the rainbow Bifrost, which bridges earth and Asgard, the Norse home of the gods.

Maxfield Frederick Parrish · *Hill Top* · United States · 1926 One of the most famous painters of his time, Parrish gave idyllic landscapes an undeniable spirit and light. He said the women under the tree were "in quiet contemplation of the environment," as their faces befittingly express.

Massimo Scolari
Urban Passage Project: Axonometric · Italy
1974 Surreal and asymmetrical, the watercolor exhibits Scolari's architectural interpretation of a house that defies standard building norms, which liberated the artist from confined ideology.

(opposite, top) Johann Wilhelm Baur · *Jacob's Dream* · Germany · 17th Century Biblical patriarch Jacob dreams of a ladder to heaven of which angels ascend and descend bearing communications from God for humans, in the tempura and parchment visual of the famed story.

(opposite, bottom) Sandro Botticelli · *The Abyss of Hell* · Italy · 1480s Dante's Divine Comedy version of the inferno was one of many illustrations in the original manuscript considered masterpieces. His rendition is a vertical cone presenting the descent of Dante and Virgil through the nine circles of Hell.

Unknown · *Utopian City* · Hungary · 1922
Published in *Aller Lapja* magazine, the panoramic
cover illustration comes from an architectural article.

Eugène Ernest Hillemacher · *Psyche in the Underworld*
France · 1865 One of the tasks assigned to
Psyche by Venus, was to retrieve a jar containing
Persephone's beauty. The artist depicts the scene
just before Psyche, despite warnings not to open the
receptacle, cannot control her desire to peer inside.

(opposite) Jean Giraud
(Moebius) · *Arzak and
the Rock* · France · 1995
Moebius' comic strip
series of the 1970s,
Arzach, featured a hero
who rides on a stone
bird. They journey
across wastelands and
futuristic desert land-
scapes and other wild
terrain, conveying a
mysterious purpose for
their adventures.

Zaha Hadid · *Vitra
Fire Station design
study* · Iraq · 1990
The conceptual,
architectural drawing
is meant to transmit
cultural shifts in
response to social
change. Like the
Archigram movement,
the images influence
alternative thought
and merge spaces for
a more integrated
aesthetic and sense of
wonder. The sculpture-
esque Vitra Fire Station
gives viewers a sense
of spatial oddity.

Disney Studio Artist · *Concept drawing for Fantasia*
Denmark · 1940 The final scene of *Fantasia* takes
place on Walpurgis night, which presents the conflict
between the profane and the sacred and features
the composition by Modest Mussorgsky and Franz
Schubert.

Stephanie Law · *Avalon* · United States · 2013
Lush and fantastical, the mythic sword Excalibur
was forged in Avalon, where it awaited its retrieval
by King Arthur. Thought to bear a likeness to
Glastonbury, the isle rises from a marshy lake and
symbolizes a place of magic and rebirth of the self.

(opposite)
William Blake · *Satan calling up his Legions, from John Milton's 'Paradise Lost'* · England ca. 1805 Blake often painted scenes from spiritual texts, literature and myth and was particularly enamored of the works of Milton. Experimenting with the use of tempera on canvas, Blake describes his technique here as 'largely painted in glazes on top of gold leaf.' The result is a shimmering, otherworldly aesthetic.

(top) D. B. Weiss and David Benioff · *Game of Thrones* · United States · 2019 The realms depicted throughout the books of fantasy author George R. R. Martin are reinterpreted into the dramatic cinematic worlds of the popular live-action television series.

(bottom) Peter Jackson · *Still from The Hobbit: The Desolation of Smaug* · New Zealand · 2013 The director Peter Jackson reimagines the fantastic literary worlds J.R.R. Tolkien in his epically cinematic series of films.

Stanislav Szukalski
Submerged Town
Poland · 1954 "Thirst
brought him to this
waterhole in the
parched desert. While
drinking the water he
suddenly beheld a town
on the bottom of this
scoopful of water, bury-
ing his face in it to see
more, almost forgetting
to breathe, and hating
to return to this world...
this scorched, lifeless,
friendless, empty desert"
– Stanislav Szukalski

O.P.V
2003

(opposite) Guillermo Perez Villalta · *Ulises Parte de la Isla de Circe* Spain · 2003 Villata's surreal interpretation of the mythological island Aeaea, belonging to the proto-sorceress Circe, shows Ulysses' arrival to its shores to rescue his men, where he lives with her for one year.

Salvador Dalí · *The Echo of the Void* · Spain 1935 Cypress trees create a portal mirrored in the background to invoke a void of space, with the surreal possibility of veil between life and death. Dali captures a landscape of wonder and ponder in the oil on canvas.

Disney Studio Artist *Harmony* · United States · 1935 Disney's Music Land features the Land of Symphony, Sea of Dischor, and Isle of Jazz with a buildup to war, yet ends happily with a double wedding, between prince and princess, and the king and queen. The citizens of both lands dance on the newly built Bridge of Harmony with a musical note rainbow running through it.

Michael Whelan · *Mountain of Black Glass* · United
States · 1999 As cover art for Tad Williams highly
acclaimed book series, the pharaonic landscape
illustrates the cyber fantasy realm of an unfinished
land. It is presented as an epic poem ultimately
leading to an immortal future.

Rick Guidice
*Retrofuturistic NASA
Space Art* · United
States · 1970s
Colonization of space
has long been a con-
cept, one that warranted
study and rendering
by the NASA Ames
Research Center. The
toroidal cityscape was
created in poster form
to help connect the
public to the scientific
potential as a tool
for exploration and
discovery.

Denis Villeneuve
Blade Runner 2049
Canada · 2017 An
apocalyptic, futuristic
world is imaginatively
depicted throughout
the *Blade Runner*
science fiction franchise
of books and films.

Hieronymus Bosch · *The Garden of Earthly Delights*
Spain · 1490–1500 The triptych of beasts and
humans abounds with Bosch's signature fantastical
and conceptual style. Oftentimes, his work depicts
religious stories like the temptation and the fall in
the famed garden.

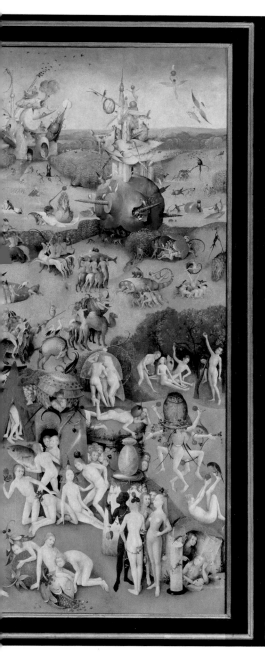

(top) Tuco Amalfi
Love and Empathy
Brazil · 2005 His belief
that art is a gift from
God and should be
done in his service, is
imparted through the
beauty and energy
exuded from his paint-
ings. He says, "In the
background we are all
the same, the same we
are in the background
in our being where love
is the center, where God
is the power."

James Cameron · *Na'vi Worship at the Tree of Souls*
Canada · *2022 Avatar: The Way of Water* film still
lights up the ritual of the sapient species in reverence
to the tall, bioluminescent tree with which they connect and communicate to the God, Eywa.

(opposite) Brendan Pattengale · *Wait A Lifetime*
United States · 2022 With a focus on striking
geological features, intense color, and interesting
photographic methods, Pattengale travels to the
farthest reaches of the world to capture untouched
landscapes with mythical proportions.

Mary Blair · *Concept drawings for Walt Disney's Alice in Wonderland* · United States · 1951 Alice's fall down the psychedelic rabbit hole portrays the idea of traversing a portal into another reality. The conceptual rendition focuses on the bright splash of reflection, like a specter of the wildness she was about to encounter.

Frank Frazetta · *New World* · United States · 1972
The 1972 Annual World's Best Science Fiction cover
featured one of Franzetta's fantasy-styled scenes of
futuristic worlds. Recognized internationally, his work
has graced books, comics, album covers and more.

There is something quite powerful in activating the luminous temples, the inner landscapes of our imagination, the sacred spaces that reveal the collective beneficent potentiality of our species, indeed all sentient life here on Mother Earth and beyond. I am a novelist and a creator of media that catalyzes consciousness: Media as Medicine for our times. My practice is the evocation of the sacred inner and outer land-scapes, the reigniting of our potentiality as a species to live deeply into our essential interconnectivity with each other and all life to remem-ber our potential to create beneficent cultures and civilizations. The novels are crafted to activate the inner transcultural mythic memory through regenerative myths, stories, and sacred sites, recasting history to include the mystery and magick of long-forgotten feminine lineage lines. For me, the transcultural pilgrimage, finding the mystical thread of connection across sacred sites and traditions, has been a primary catalysis and inspiration. I have found remembrance and solace in the high mountain yogi caves and temples of Bhutan and Tibet; the temples and tea gardens of Kyoto, the ghats of the Ganges, the sacred spiral and waters of Glastonbury, the cathedrals of the ancient redwoods; and the vast open deserts of the North American Southwest where the sea of stars reflect on natural cathedrals of sand and stone. I have found remembrance in the cobbled streets and cathedrals of Paris, the intricately carved stone temples of Bali, and the hundred-foot-high waterfalls of Kauai. As humans, we are a sacred site, a cosmogram coming to life through our pilgrimage and remembrance of the living Codex of our Mother Earth. As a species, humanity is at a pivotal moment where, to avert collective catastrophe, we have the opportunity to transform our inner sacred landscapes, the imaginal realms of possibility, and the myths and stories that are the DNA of our civilizations. Of all the worlds of possibilities, why not make this beneficent future possible, civilizations and temples built in testimony to the sacredness of all sentient life? This is not only our potential but the way forward. Let's create our Sacred Sites, the Temples of Our Future!

— SARAH DREW, Artist, Social Philosopher, and Author
of the multi-volume *Gaia Codex Series*, 2024

(opposite) Aqa Mirak
*The Ascent of the Prophet
Mohammed on his Mount*
Iran · 1543 Intricately
illustrated, the manu-
script of the Khamsa
(five poems) of Nizami
Ganjavi was created
for the Persian emperor
and is one of the most
notable works of Persian
literature. The artist
Mirak portrays a flying
Mohammad being
escorted by Jibra'il and
a flock of angels.

Utagawa Kunisada II
The Hell Courtesan
Japan · 1850s Sur-
rounded by an extensive
scene of a Buddhist
hell realm, the King
of Hell presides on his
throne in the center of
it all on the robe of
a Japanese oiran, or
prostitute. Prostitution
was still legal in Japan
until 1958.

William Blake
Jacob's Ladder · England
1800–03 Angels
ascend and descend,
from earth to heaven
and back again, on a
ladder which appeared
to Jacob in a dream.
The symbolic and
biblical dream world is
portrayed in sparkling
detail by Blake, who
was a master at poetic
visuals.

Nicholas Roerich · *Svyatogor* · Russia · 1942
Just years before his death while living in India,
Roerich painted many Russian saints and heroes like
Svyatogor, the giant, whose weight can hardly be
supported by Mother Earth. He is portrayed amongst
the snowy mountains Roerich is famous for painting.

PARADISE FOUND

Utopias, Communes & Intentional Communities

I'm following a course that was chosen for me, following a pressing need to show that a woman can work on a monumental scale. I am creating a sort of joyland, where you could have a new kind of life that would just be free.

— NIKI DE SAINT PHALLE, Artist & Seeker,
in a letter regarding building her Tarot Garden art installation, 1981

Frida Kahlo prone in her bed, paintbrush in hand. Calder in his light-filled studio, surrounded by his creations. Georgia O'Keeffe gazing out the window of Ghost Ranch, watching the softly-muted sunsets of the New Mexico desert. An artist activates the space around them, their creative force, their aura imbued into the places they live and work, in their studios, in their gardens and into the landscapes that surround them and inspire them. In many cases, the spaces the artist occupies is art in and of itself. The fantastical hand-built homes of SunRay Kelly, the surrealist sculptural experiments of Dalí, the boldly innovative designs of architects like R. Buckminster Fuller.

There are also places ignited by communal expression, spaces constructed as a collective utopian vision. Even specific areas of a city can attract the artist through the siren song of other creatives, the bohemian cafés, and ateliers of Montmartre in Paris for instance, a neighborhood once home to Pablo Picasso,

Vincent van Gogh, and Henri de Toulouse-Lautrec. In New York City, the halls of the Chelsea Hotel have seen decades of artists, musicians, and writers, a creative, eclectic environment, muse to icons such as Bob Dylan, Andy Warhol, Patti Smith, and Leonard Cohen. Greenwich Village in New York, at the height of the 1960s folk scene, Santa Teresa in Rio de Janeiro, or Christiania in Copenhagen, these are all neighborhoods and communities born of the vibrant creative expressions of the people that live there.

Communes and collective living experiments created by counterculture philosophies are another form of sacred spaces—landscapes made unique through focused and united intent. In the American Southwest, the experimental city of Arcosanti was the dream of Italian American architect Paolo Soleri. Building began in 1970 and represented his vision of a concept he termed "arcology," a mix of "architecture" and "ecology." Arcology is aimed at achieving urban

Eric Schaal · *Entrance and ticket booth of the "Dream of Venus" exhibition* · Germany · 1939 Designed for the 1939 World's Fair in New York, the Salvador Dalí interpretation of a funhouse became a surrealist exhibit of grand proportion. The fascinating dreamscape gave fairgoers a sensory experience of the highest degree.

structures that are efficient and sustainable. The design of Arcosanti includes innovations such as large, sun-shaded windows to maximize the capture of solar heat, and energy-efficient systems that use passive solar heating and cooling. A work-in-progress since its inception, Arcosanti is designed to eventually house a population of several thousand people and currently serves as an ongoing exploration into the feasibility of Soleri's arcology and ecological ideals.

In the early 1960s, another utopian experiment was founded by a group of American art students seeking an alternate way of building and creating. Drop City was the result, a community known for its distinctive dome-shaped structures built from salvaged materials, including scrapped car roofs and other industrial refuse. The community became a countercultural icon and a symbol of the "back-to-the-land" movement of the 1960s and 1970s, promoting values of peace, free love, and harmony with the environment. Drop City was not only a living space but also a collaborative artistic environment that pursued the creation of "Drop Art," which was inspired by the concept of "dropping works of art" into a wide variety of natural and urban settings. Many of the community's structures were inspired by the work of Buckminster Fuller and his embrace of the geodesic dome as the architecture of the future. The concept of the geodesic dome was popularized by Fuller, a 20th-century inventor, architect, and futurist, who sought to create efficient and sustainable designs.

The utopian space can also translate to the artists' studios themselves, the creative creating and curating their homes as another expression of their work. The Californian artist and photographer Steven Arnold lived and created in his expansive, sumptuously decorated Los Angeles studio, a place he dubbed "Zanzibar". Throughout the 1980s and early 1990s, Arnold hosted parties and salons and staged intricately ornate tableaus where he posed his models and muses in fantastical costumes and make-up. The musician Alice Coltrane created a collective community in the hills of Malibu, California, where she taught music and meditation, raising her children amid the sound of birdsong, harp, and sacred chanting. The counterculture icon, artist, and witch, Vali Myers discovered her personal paradise in the early 1970s in Positano, Italy, taking up residence in a secluded valley where she lived among her vast menagerie of animals, creating poetry and paintings. Some creators literally live inside their own artworks, such as the remarkable "sculpture as residence" built by the California woodworker J.B. Blunk or Salvador Dalí's whimsical seaside abode at Portlligat, Spain. Perhaps the most expressive of these sacred artist spaces is Tuscany's Tarot Garden, the wildly imaginative creation and one-time home of the artist Niki de Saint Phalle. A monumental accomplishment, Saint Phalle's sculpture garden features the Tarot's Major Arcana expressed as enormous statuary. The largest, a magical mirror ball interpretation of the Empress card, was built with a kitchen and living area inside her belly, a space which Saint Phalle occupied for several years—an artist inhabiting her own work, an intimate union between creation and creator.

Randy Harris · *SunRay Kelley* · United States 2012 A legend in the world of alternative building and designing, SunRay Kelley stands in front of his Garden House in Washington State. On his nine-acre homestead, Kelley built seven houses, ten ponds, a hermit's hut, and a seventeen-foot-tall maple-wood Jesus.

USCO · *'Be-In'*
At Riverside Museum,
New York · United
States · 1966 One
of the many artworks
created in the 1960s
by a group calling
itself USCO (an
abbreviation for "the
Us Company").
A collective of artists
and engineers, USCO
staged interactive,
acid-inspired art
shows in galleries and
museums around the
United States.

Leslie Williamson · *Sunrise at the JB Blunk house*
United States · 2022 The Blunk House was built by
artist J.B. Blunk in 1959–62 in Inverness, California,
using salvaged redwood. Some of his most well
known artworks were made on site in his studio.

Peter Granser
El Alto, ID20461514
Germany · 2015
Vibrant buildings post
along the Bolivian town,
El Alto. Derived from
indigenous Aymara
culture, bricklayer
turned architect Freddy
Mamani created what
he calls New Andean
Architecture. The aes-
thetic has transformed
the city as a social and
economic expression
of the Aymara people.

(following pages)
Various · *Osaka Expo*
Japan · 1970 With a
theme of "Progress and
Harmony for Humanity,"
one of the largest and
most visited exhibitions
in history included
geodesic domes, the
first IMAX film, a moon
rock display, magnetic
levitation and the first
ever mobile phones.

(opposite, top) Ernest and Ruth Norman · *Star Center* · United States · 2015 Unarius, (or Universal Articulate Interdimensional Understanding of Science), was founded in 1954. The murals at the Star Center, depict the civilization of Atlantis at its zenith, 37,000 years ago.

(opposite, bottom) Peter Jon Pearce · *Biosphere 2* United States · 1991 Built on a little over three acres, the Biosphere experiment aimed to further ecological understanding and find sustainable solutions for the planet and people, by simulating biosystems enclosed in glass.

Kisho Kurokawa · *The Takara Beautilion* · Japan
1970 Within the phenomenal Osaka Expo is a symbolic tower meant to convey "the joy of being beautiful." The Takara Beautilion's award winning architecture by Kisho Kurokawa instilled hope for the future with its mind-blowing modular design.

Alfredo J. Martiz J. · *Nakagin Capsule Tower*
Panama · 2007 As the first ever example of capsule architecture, the Kisho Kurokawa tower in Japan was built for actual, mixed use. It stood from its inception in 1972 until modern building management decided to demolish it in 2022.

(following pages)
Yann Arthus-Bertrand
*Moshav (co-operative
village) farm at Nahalal,
Jezrael plain, Israel
(32°41' N, 35°13' E)*
France · Date Unknown
Established in 1971, the
moshav farms became
ideal communities for
new immigrants who
were used to communal
style living with pooled
labor and resources,
similar to the
kibbutz model with
small differences in
ownership specifics.

(opposite)
Matthias Dengler
The Goetheanum
Germany · 2019
Designed by Rudolf
Steiner and named
after Goethe, the
Goetheanum building
in Dornach, Switzerland,
is characterized by non-
conforming architectural
building plans. Avoiding
right angles, he com-
missioned boat builders
to fashion the rounded
forms that define much
of the shapes in the
picturesque world center
for the anthroposophi-
cal movement.

Jerry de Wilde · *Chumash Indian Wedding Ceremony/
The Farm* · United States · 1970 Photographer de
Wilde captures a celebratory wedding circle held in
the fields at The Farm, a legendary commune and
collective in Los Angeles.

Robert L. McElroy · *Multimedia Event in The USCO
Tabernacle* · United States · 1966 The "Us Company"
was founded by poet Gerd Stern and filmmaker
Judi Stern with a group of artists, poets, filmmakers,
engineers, and composers who formed a coopera-
tive space in a church in Garnerville, New York.

(opposite, top)
Paolo Soleri
The Vaults at Arcosanti
United States
1971–75 A synthesis of
ecology and architec-
ture form the basis of
arcology, of which the
800-acre Arcosanti is
an impressive example.
Meant to support and
sustain radically shifting
climates and culture, the
Paolo Solari creation
has been evolving for
over fifty years.

(opposite, bottom)
Alex & Allyson Grey
*Entheon, Sanctuary of
Visionary Art at the
Chapel of Sacred Mirrors*
United States · 2008
Visionary artists Alex
and Allyson Grey
created an upstate New
York artist sanctum as
a display venue for
psychedelic expression.
It serves as an interfaith
church and features
artwork from the
couple as well as other
consciousness-
expanding creators.

Charles Eames · *Eames House* · United States
1949 Known as Case Study House No. 8, the
Charles and Ray Eames mid-century, De Stijl styled
and designed home was part of a program to
design chic, modern homes on a budget. The iconic
style had a huge impact in the world of design.

Frederic Edwin Church · *Olana Court Hall Interior*
United States · 1872 Famed Hudson River landscape painter Frederic Church built a persian-
inspired mansion on a scenic hilltop in Hudson,
New York, as a gift to his wife.

Unknown · *Sunburst Sanctuary* · United States 1978 Known as 'The Brotherhood of the Sun,' the intentional community began what would become a thriving center for spirituality. Just north of Santa Barbara, California, the 160-acre ranch was the largest organic farm in America.

Clark Richert · *The Ultimate Painting* · United States · 1966 The abstract kaleidoscopic canvas was painted for the dome of Drop City. It was lost in 1969 but recreated in 2011 by Richert with help from artists Richard Kallweit, JoAnn Bernofsky, Gene Bernofsky, and Charles DiJulio.

Mirra Alfassa and Roger Anger *Matrimandir* · India 2008 The daybreak photo captures the elevated spiritual utopia of influential Indian philosopher and yogi Sri Aurobindo. Dedicated to the universal Mother, the glass dome in the center is the inner sanctum, meant for mediation and set upon twelve symbolic pillars of direction and aspects of the Great Mother.

(following pages) Drop City · *"The Complex" Trinidad, Colorado* · United States ca. 1966 Southern Colorado was the home of the counterculture artist community called Drop City, which began as a response to material-bound society. The rural commune was built based on the dome design of Buckminster Fuller using mostly found materials for almost no cost.

Lawrence Schiller
Dancing Pranksters
United States · 1966
A prolific photographer,
Schiller often turns his
lens onto key moments
of popular culture,
capturing here explo-
rations in psychedelic
art and early immersive
experiments in dance,
environment, and L.S.D.

Jack Garofalo
The Cockettes · France
1971 Part commune,
part performance
troupe, The Cockettes
were a vibrant, ongoing
experiment in dance,
fluidity of sexual
identity, and collective
artmaking.

Unknown · *Alice Coltrane* · **United States** · **1970**
The iconic jazz legend Alice Coltrane fearlessly
explored the boundaries of music, art, and spiritual
teachings, leading an ashram collective which
taught communal chanting, meditation, and music,
to a generation of students.

BIG - Bjarke Ingels Group · *The Orb* Denmark · 2018 Made from thirty tons of steel and fifteen thousand hours of sewing, the eighty-foot diameter mirrored orb visually reflects the entirety of Black Rock City, which hosts the annual Burning Man cultural movement in the Nevada desert.

Satellite photo · *Aerial View of The Burning Man Festival* · United States · 2012 Urban planner Rod Garrett designed the crescent-shaped Black Rock City, home to Burning Man on a Nevada playa. The design has remained since its inception and requires an enormous amount of organization to support the eighty thousand attendees.

(opposite) Giulio Romano, Giambattista Scultori, & Michele Sanmicheli *Fireplace at Villa Della Torre* · Italy · ca. 1560 Built for Giulio Della Torre in Fumane, the villa is filled with mon-ster-mouthed fireplaces. From the gardens to the rooms inside, the mas-terpiece design exudes a complex symbolism and spiritual meaning.

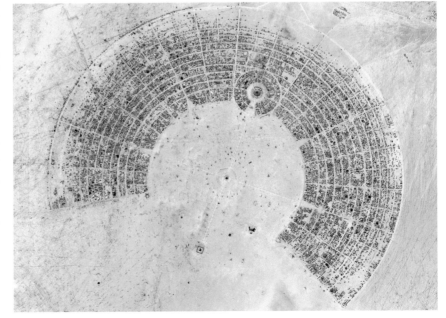

Evans · *Alexander Calder* · **United States ca. 1955** Using tin, steel and wire, sculptor Calder's abstract constructions fill his studio with mobile wonder. The artist ventured into large scale sculptures which stand as public installations all over the world.

405

Tony Vaccaro · *Georgia O'Keeffe in Her Ranch* United States · 1960 In the remote high-desert plateau of northern New Mexico, the artist sits in her adobe-built Ghost Ranch. About the land, which was thought to be haunted, she says it's "Such a beautiful, untouched lonely feeling place, such a fine part of what I call the 'Faraway.'"

Unknown · *Hilma af Klint at the Kungliga Akademien in Stockholm* Sweden · 1885
Painter of predictions, astral esoterics and spiritual wonderment, Theosophical and Anthroposophical devotee, Hilma af Klint work was not publicly recognized until 1986, decades after her death. She said of her work, "In carrying out this life's work, it was to be an Anthroposophist as best I could… I understand that I did not make myself understood."

(opposite) Steven
Arnold · *Self-Portrait*
United States · 1986
In his 'Zanzibar' studio,
the multidisciplinary
Dalí protogé poses
amongst vintage
collectibles and animal
print decor. It is here
where he created his
later works, like the
assemblage sculptures
and tableau-vivants for
which he was known.

Ben Buchanan
*Jean-Michael Basquiat
painting 'Pree' at Area*
United States · 1985
Jazz great Charlie
Parker's daughter Pree
is the subject in a few
of Basquiat's saxophon-
ist series paintings, in
which he painted scenes
and words based on
his favorite players.
The capture shows the
artist in process.

(previous pages)
Hervé Gloaguen · *Andy Warhol in New York* France · 1966 Parisian photographer, Hervé Gloaguen, shot the Warhol crew including Nico, Gérard Malanga, and Paul Morrissey, in what was Andy Warhol's most iconic and cool period. His famous factory teemed with counterculture figures as both subjects and those behind the camera.

Unknown · *R. Buckminster Fuller, creator of the geodesic dome* · United States · 1968 Surrounded with examples of his famed structures, American architect, systems theorist, author, designer, inventor and futurist, Fuller sits in his office in Carbondale, Illinois.

David Montgomery · *David Hockney* · United States · 1988 The saturated palettes of California scenery define Hockney's signature mixed style. The English painter moved to Los Angeles in the 60's, using the west coast color palette as a source of inspiration.

(opposite) Unknown
Salvador Dalí and Gala
Spain · 1957 Spanish
surrealist, Dalí, poses
with his wife and muse,
Gala, who was the
subject of many of his
works. Their home in
Port Lligat is now a
tourist destination and
a wonderful experience
of the imaginative living
space of a legend.

Karl Bissinger · *Henry
Miller* · United States
1950 Bissinger docu-
mented author Henry
Miller in photo and writ-
ing, visiting him in his
Big Sur, California res-
idence in which Miller
found "grandeur and
eloquent silence" when
it was still a remote and
quiet paradise. He is
credited with populariz-
ing tourism there.

Michel Sima
Jean Cocteau · Poland
1955 After striking up
a companionship with
Francine Weisweiller,
Cocteau spent time in
her Santo Sospir villa on
the Cote d'Azur where
he painted over two
hundred mythological
images from Greek,
Roman and biblical
murals on the walls.

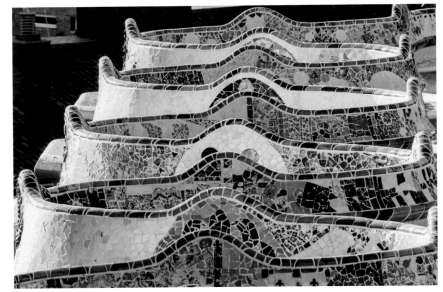

(previous, left) Yousef Karsh · *Carl Jung in his office* · Canada · 1958 Jung's symbolic stained-glass study where he created 'The Red Book' is a very small, dark room. It is said that while he was in this personal space, he only allowed two reasons to be disturbed: war or fire.

(previous, right) Gisèle Freund · *Frida Kahlo Painting in Her Bedroom* France · 1951 Kahlo's debilitating injuries often required periods of being bed-ridden, which did not stop her from creating. She hung a mirror above her bed, and with a custom-made easel continued to paint the self-portraits she was known for.

(top) Antoni Gaudí *Bench at Park Güell* Spain · 1926 World famous Park Güell bench in the Antoni Gaudí designed garden city was referred to as a precursor of surrealism by Salvador Dalí. The iconic snake-like seat imparts a whimsical tone and has a spectacular view of the city below.

Dennis Hopper · *Niki de St. Phalle* · United States 1967 Hopper shot many portraits of his friends, enabling him to intimately capture them in process. Sculptor, painter, filmmaker, and author, Phalle is shot painting one of her sculptures.

(opposite) Niki de Saint Phalle · *The Chapel at The Tarot Garden* · France/United States · 2011 Saint Phalle designed a fantastically psychedelic tarot garden in the Tuscan countryside. Twenty-two large scale mosaic major arcana figures fill the landscape, fusing naturally with the surrounding vegetation.

ART AS WORSHIP

Theaters, Museums & Libraries

The only thing that you absolutely have to know, is the location of the library.

— ALBERT EINSTEIN, Theoretical Physicist, 1912

Art as an act of transcendence, of spiritual seeking—this is what imbues a space with sacredness. In this way, perhaps the great libraries, museums and theaters of the world are indelibly marked by the resonance of the creativity they hold within. Think of the dancers and singers who have graced the stages at the Bolshoi in Moscow or the Metropolitan Opera House in New York City or at La Scala in Milan. Imagine the host of renowned musicians who have played the Royal Albert Hall in London since it first opened in 1871 or the performances that took place at the Theatre of Dionysus in Athens, Greece. Dating back to the 6th century BCE, this site is often considered the first theater in the world, built in honor of the god Dionysus, and holding up to 15,000 spectators at its peak.

The Greek were perhaps the first culture to erect spaces for art and performance. The Epidaurus Theatre in the Peloponnese, Greece, constructed in the 4th century BCE, is one of the best-preserved of their many ancient theaters. The Roman's also built structures dedicated to gathering for public spectacle, such as the Roman Theatre of Orange in France, built early in the 1st century. The latter is one of the best-preserved of these Roman theaters and is still in use today. The Aspendos Theatre in Turkey was constructed during the reign of Marcus Aurelius and is famous for exquisitely ornate stage, a beautiful example of Roman theater architecture that remains intact and still hosts performances throughout the year.

Museums, as well, hold a unique allure as creative sacred sites. The energy imbued within these spaces is ignited perhaps by a dedication to showcasing great paintings and sculpture, with patrons immersed in the awe which comes from worshiping at the great altar of art. How many have stood in front of DaVinci's *Mona Lisa* at the Louvre Museum in Paris and been transformed? Or found elation in viewing an El Greco at Madrid's Prado Museum? The British Museum in London holds a vast collection of artifacts, thousands of objects which record the history of humanity

(previous)
André Breton · *The Wall* · France · 1966 Dada writer and surrealist movement founder, André Breton had an extensive collection of artifacts that ranged a full spectrum of wonder. Displayed on a wall in his studio and later moved to the Centre Pompidou, the visual seemed to be an active metaphor or spatial representation of his belief systems and rejection of typified art displays.

Sir John Soane · *The domed gallery at the Soane Museum* · England · 1807 Sir John Sloane turned his home into a museum filled with innumerable relics from ancient Greek, Roman, and Egyptian empires, including Old Master paintings, drawings, and rare books, so that all may have access to the brilliance of the old world.

and its creations of art and culture. The Metropolitan Museum of Art in New York houses an extensive collection spanning various cultures and time periods—statues from ancient Egypt are displayed alongside jewelry from ancient Greece—the gods and goddesses of antiquity standing sentinel amid the bustle of the modern age. New York's Guggenheim Museum, established by philanthropist Solomon R. Guggenheim and art advisor Hilla von Rebay, began in the late 1920s with acquisition of works by artists, including Wassily Kandinsky and Piet Mondrian. In the 1940s, Guggenheim met architect Frank Lloyd Wright and commissioned him to design a new museum to house the growing collection. Construction of the now iconic spiral-shaped building began in 1956 and the museum opened to the public in 1959. It has since become one of the most famous and influential institutions in the world, known for its architectural significance and innovative approach to showcasing art. In October of 2018, the Guggenheim Museum opened the exhibit, "Hilma af Klint: Paintings for the Future," a groundbreaking retrospective of the Swedish artist. The show featured over 170 of af Klint's works, including her vibrant large-scale paintings that predate the abstract art movements of the 20th century. Af Klint's art was marked by her interest in spiritualism, theosophy, and the exploration of the unseen and cosmic realms. Nearly a hundred years prior to the extensive Guggenheim show, af Klint, in her early writings, envisioned a large, spiral-shaped building in which to display what she called her, "temple paintings."

The Dalí Theatre-Museum (Teatro-Museo Dalí), located in Figueres, Spain, is perhaps one of the most magickal of these temples to art and one of the most significant and popular museums dedicated to a single artist. With the construction of the building overseen by Dalí himself, the museum is located in the artist's hometown and built upon the remains of the former Theatre of Figueres, which was destroyed at the end of the Spanish Civil War. The symbolism of building the museum on the theater's site is profound, as Dalí intended it to be a place where art, theatricality, and surrealism meet. The museum was inaugurated in 1974 and includes a significant number of works that Dalí contributed during his lifetime. True to the nature of Dalí's art, the museum itself is a piece of surrealist masterwork and features numerous symbolic elements (such as the egg and loaf of bread) that were recurring motifs in his artwork. Dalí is also buried there, in a crypt deep beneath the stage floor. Not merely a collection of the artist's work, the museum is a monument to the artist himself, a testament to his vision and creativity and a pilgrimage site for those fascinated by Dalí's work.

The idea of a collective art space as sacred site, is perhaps most resonate within the great libraries of the world, enormous repositories of knowledge and ideas that have existed for centuries throughout global cultures. The Library of Alexandria, founded in the 3rd century BCE in Alexandria, Egypt, was one of the largest and most significant libraries of the ancient world. Although it did not survive, its legacy has influenced the

(following pages)
Thomas H. Shepherd
Bullock's Museum
England · 1810 In a series of Volumes titled 'The Survey of London,' documenting London's past and current history of architectural building, the Egyptian Hall in Piccadilly, also called Bullock's Museum, housed William Bullock's collection of relics brought back by Captain Cook from his adventures and more.

Domenico Sciassia · *Vorau Abbey Library*
Switzerland/Austria · 1731 The library at the baroque Stift Vorau monastery in Austria was filled with precious Augustinian books, many of

which were burned in a fire, destroyed by Nazi regime takeover, and stolen over time. Still, it remains a sacred archive full of beauty and history.

BULLOC

Plate 35. Vol. 3.

(following pages)
Domenico Remps
Cabinet of Curiosities
Germany/Italy · 1690s
Collecting relics was a
pastime of great import
during the seventeenth
century, as a way to
understand life and
make sense of the
world, captured in oil on
canvas by Remps as a
document to the trend.

and houses extensive collections of books, manuscripts, and prints. The Bodleian Library in Oxford, England it is one of the oldest libraries in Europe and holds a large collection of ancient manuscripts. In Dublin, Trinity College Library is the largest library in Ireland and houses the famous *Book of Kells*, an illuminated manuscript dating back to the 9th century.

Then there are the collections of the esoteric—the occult, the alchemical manuscripts, and mysterious spell book grimoires. The arcana of the oldest existing Tarot cards, their hand-painted symbology etched onto antique vellum, are scattered throughout the world, held in various archives such as The Morgan in New York City and the Beinecke Rare Book & Manuscript Library at Yale University. One of the world's largest libraries devoted entirely to rare books and manuscripts, the Beinecke holds a copy of the *Gutenberg Bible*, the first Western book printed from movable type, and the mysterious *Voynich Manuscript*, an illustrated codex hand-written in an unknown writing system which has yet to be deciphered.

development of libraries throughout history and around the globe. The Al-Qarawiyyin Library, part of the Al-Qarawiyyin University in Fez, Morocco, was first established in 859 AD. Often referred to as the oldest existing continuously operating institution in the world, the library holds a significant collection of Islamic manuscripts.

The Vatican Apostolic Library, established in 1475 in Rome, it is also sometimes considered the oldest library in the world in terms of continuity, since it has been operating without interruption since inception. The British Library in London, England, holds a vast collection of books, manuscripts, and historic documents, including the *Magna Carta*. The Bibliothèque nationale de France, France's national library, is situated in Paris

The magick of the theater, of watching actors embody the great human journey, or pulling leatherbound books from the shelves while exploring the vast archives of the world's great libraries, or bowing low in front of masterpieces, amid the houses of creative worship we call museums—all these acts express is a kind of spiritual expansion—a direct way to connect with the divine alchemy of creation itself.

Unknown · *Manly P. Hall at his library the Philosophical Research Society in Los Feliz* · United States · 1985 One of the most rare and valuable esoteric and occult collections amassed in recent history, the library of the philosopher Manly P. Hall lives on at the Philosophical Research Society.

Dr. Henry C. Mercer · *Fonthill Castle* · United States · 1912 The archeologist, collector, and self-taught ceramicist Henry Chapman Mercer created his own experimental architecture with his whimsical Fonthill Castle in Pennsylvania.

Unknown · *New York Philharmonic at the Bowl* United States · 1963 Leonard Bernstein leads the orchestra at the Hollywood Bowl. There are seats now where there was once a reflection pool which gave the Bowl a stunning mirrored effect.

Alfred Waterhouse *The Central Hall of the Natural History Museum* England · 1882 One year after it was opened to the public, the symmetrical beauty of the central hall in the London Natural History Museum is captured in its grandeur.

(opposite) C. Gel *Interior of the Small Theatre or Odeon, Pompeii* · Italy · 1898 The chromolithograph from *Antonio Niccoliniõs, Pompeii: Views and Restorations* aims to recreate pre-volcanic illustration of audiences in the theater.

(following pages) Ivan Bilibin · *Decor for the Opera 'Sadko'* · Russia 1914 Sketches of the scenery for Nikolai Rimsky-Korsakov's famed opera come to life in watercolor, depicting frescoes of the story.

433

И. БИЛИБИНЪ. 1914.

435

(opposite, top)
Unknown · *The Globe
Theatre* · England · 20th
Century Shakespeare's
historic playhouse,
The Globe, was an
outdoor theatre with a
centralized yard open to
the sky. The illustration
shows the first version
that burnt down and
was replaced by a brick
variant.

(opposite, bottom)
Edgar Degas · *The Ballet
Scene from 'Robert le
Diable' by Meyerbeer*
France · 1876 Consid-
ered one of the most
successful in the history
of operas, 'Robert
the Devil' surged with
symbolism and deeply
archetypal human
experience. French
impressionist Degas
depicts the treasured
classic in his masterful
ability to portray dance.

Henri de Toulouse-
Lautrec · *At the Opera
Ball* · France · 1893
Toulouse-Lautrec
vibrantly documented
the colorful Parisian
culture of his era, the
music and dance of his
times contained within
his expressive work.

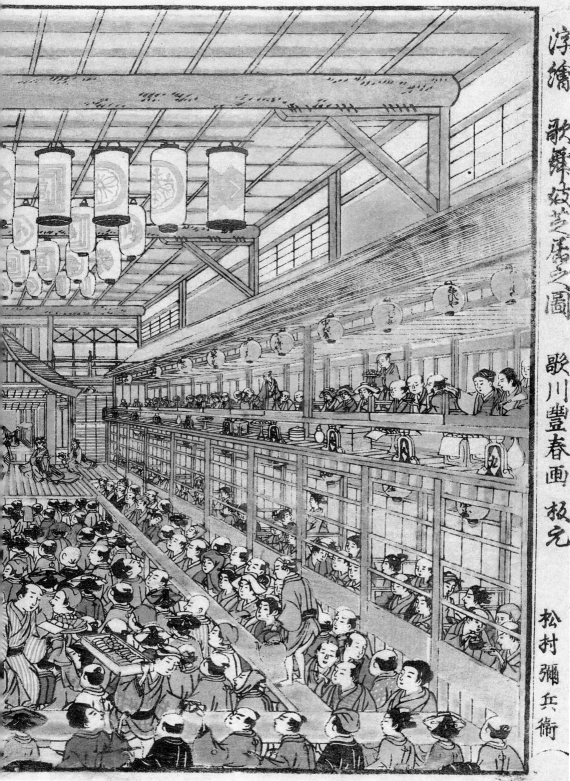

浮繪 歌舞妓芝居之圖

歌川豐春画 板元

松村彌兵衞

(previous pages)
Utagawa Toyoharu
*Perspective Picture of a
Kabuki Theater* · Japan
1776 Kabuki, roughly
translating to 'avant-
garde' portrays ordinary
life and historical events
through dance and
drama. Theaters are
staged based on cardi-
nal direction and have
sophisticated machinery,
including lifts, traps,
a rotating stage, and
much more dynamic
functionality.

Thomas Burgh · *Long Room Library, Trinity College*
Ireland · 1732 Filled with marble busts and grand
arched shelving sections, the Long Room in the
Old library at Trinity was designed by Thomas
Burgh and is home to the medieval 'Brian Boru
Harp,' a national symbol of Ireland.

Unknown · *Christ Church Hall, Oxford University*
England · 1520s Featured in many movies, such
as, *Harry Potter, The Golden Compass, X-Men: First
Class*, and the TV detective series *Endeavor*, the six-
teenth century hammer-beamed interior is delight-
fully drawn in the unknown lithograph.

(previous pages)
Giovanni Paolo Panini
Ancient Rome · Italy
1754–57 Commis-
sioned by Count Étienne
François de Choiseul,
Panini painted three
versions of the work
which depicts the
gallery of paintings
he owns. Included in
this vast collection are
paintings of The Pan-
theon, the Colosseum,
Trajan's Column, and
the Laocoön.

(following pages)
Massimo Listri
*Library of the Stiftsbiblio-
thek Sankt Gallen,
Switzerland* · Italy
2002 Switzerland's
monastic, Rococo style
library designed by
Austrian master builder,
Peter Thumb, is one of
the oldest and most
exquisite. Holding
important medieval and
modern manuscripts,
its sublime burnished
woodwork, *nouveau*
balconies and ceiling
frescoes display the
historic works with utter
glory. It was designated
a UNESCO World
Heritage site.

I.M. Pei · *Museum of Islamic Art, Qatar* · China
2008 Designed by I.M. Pei, the Doha Museum
includes a five-story main building with an education wing and a large central courtyard.

Pierre-Auguste Renoir · *At the Theatre* · France
1877 Two women watch from opera boxes in a
large theater in oil on canvas. One of three paintings by Renoir of the same subject matter featuring
theater life and fashion in Parisian culture at the time.

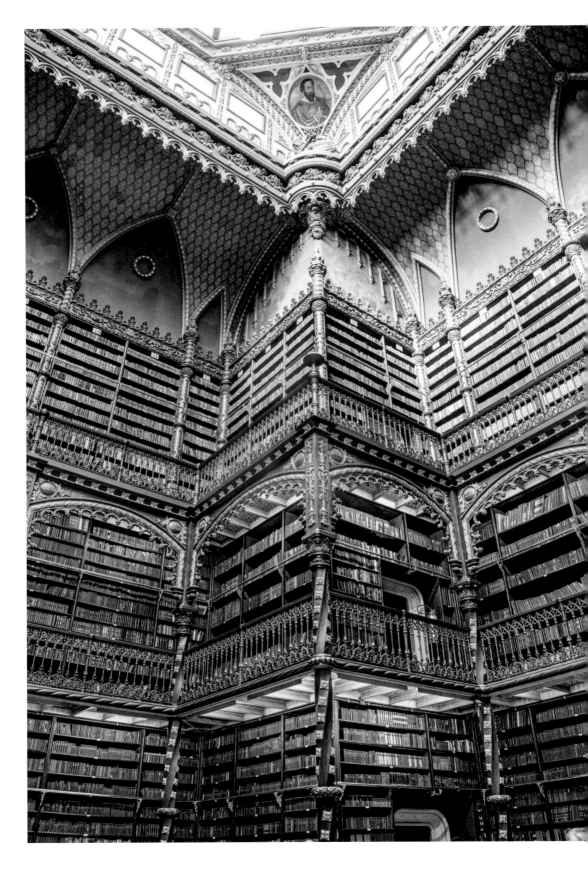

In my photography work I am always led by my own interest and curiosity in a person and their work and life. All just flows from there. I tend to enjoy the uniqueness of spaces more than the commonalities, so my mind is filled with that—how each artist creates their own perfect space to nurture their creativity. There are spaces that I've documented that resonate to me personally. Wharton Esherick's home was a place I wanted to visit for years before I finally photographed it in my first book, Handcrafted Modern. *It did not disappoint. I visit every time I am in the Philadelphia area. Alvar Aalto's Home also felt really special to me too. I could live there, which is a rare statement for me. In my own home and creative space, I like to have one little nugget from an artist/person whose home I have photographed. It's not always possible, most of the time that is in the form of books, but I do have some artwork by some the artists whose homes I have photographed, like Kay Sekimachi and J.B. Blunk. Other than that, my creative space evolves with the project I am on. It gets deconstructed at the end of a project and then slowly repopulates with the new, generally in the form of specific bits of ephemera that inspire me to keep moving forward.*

— LESLIE WILLIAMSON

Photographer, Traveler, & Author of *Handcrafted Modern: At Home with Mid-century Designers, Still Lives: In the Homes of Artists, Great and Unsung,* & *Modern Originals: At Home with MidCentury European Designers,* 2024

(following pages) Sydney Smirke · *British Library Reading Room* England · 1857 The historic, glass-domed space in the heart of the great court of the British Museum, was inspired by the domed pantheon in Rome. As an architectural marvel, the library currently archives 25,000 books, catalogs and other printed matter focusing on world cultures.

Rafael da Silva e Castro · *The Royal Portuguese Cabinet of Reading* · Portugal · 1887 Opened in 1887 in Rio de Janeiro, Brazil, the gothic library designed by architect Rafael da Silva e Castro, is a fantastical experience with almost 400,000 volumes, including rare manuscripts, significant literary works, and unique parchments and folios.

(top) Frank Lloyd Wright · *The Guggenheim Museum* · United States · 1959 One of his most enduring and futuristic works Frank Lloyd Wright experimented with sacred spiral shapes within New York City's Guggenheim, a beautiful temple dedicated to modern art.

(bottom) Claude Monet · *Exhibition of 'Nympheas' at the Musee de l'Orangerie* · France 1893 With massive presentation in mind, Monet designed his largest murals requiring an oval room to display his Giverny water garden inspired magnum opus. Built specifically to permanently house these works, the Orangery Museum erected curved rooms to accommodate the masterpieces.

Giuseppe Penone · *Leaves of Light—Tree* · Italy · 2016 Dappled sunlight, or "rain of light" is captured through the patterned, geometric dome of the Louvre Museum in Abu Dhabi. As a "galactic Arabic wonder," the Arab art structure aims to focus on "stories of human creativity that transcend individual cultures or civilization."

Louis Khan · *Salk Institute* · United States 1965 Louis Khan's iconic, La Jolla, California architectural wonder is the Salk Institute for Biological Studies. Salk, who developed the polio vaccine, wanted to create a sense of place for the betterment of humankind. The photo shows the beauty of its symmetrical design.

Armand Phillip Bartos, Frederick John Kiesler, and Gezer Heller · *Shrine of the Book* · United States/Hungary/Israel · 1965 A book as extraordinary as The Dead Sea Scrolls warrants an architectural spectacle, as is the white domed building called the Shrine of the Book in Jerusalem. The fragile books found in the Qumran caves are displayed for a few months at a time, then taken to specially designed rooms for rest from exposure, which takes its toll.

CORNERSTONE OF CREATIVITY

The Artist and Space

My art is grounded in the belief of one universal energy which runs through everything: from insect to man, from man to spectre, from spectre to plant from plant to galaxy. My works are the irrigation veins of this universal fluid. Through them ascend the ancestral sap, the original beliefs, the primordial accumulations, the unconscious thoughts that animate the world.

— ANA MENIETA, Artist & Seeker, from an artist statement on her *Silueta Series*, 1981

An enormous spiral of basalt loops inward through the waters of an ancient landlocked sea. Cement tunnels stand like sentries among a vast desert landscape, framing circular, telescopic views of a shifting sun, moon, and horizon. An observatory is carved into rock crater, the slow dance of light—day into dusk, into deep blue night, into dawn— encouraging meditation on the slow spin of our planet. Contemporary artworks which integrate natural environments as their canvas imbue a space with the sanctity of creation, the act of marking stones and sand and tree and leaf with the artist's intent. Andrew Goldsworthy's ephemeral works, for example, often interact with the landscape and are designed to change and evolve over time as they are exposed to the elements, to wind, rain, and sunlight. The late Cuban American artist, Ana Mendieta, known for her ground-breaking work in performance art, sculpture, and photography, often used her own body

as a canvas, exploring themes of feminism, identity, and nature. Her work remains pow-erfully potent, an artist in raw and sometimes confrontational collaboration with the earth itself, with skin and blood, flowers, water, and sand.

In the 1960s and 1970s, the emergence of Land Art, also known as the Earth Art Movement, embraced the use of organic materials and the creation of structures and forms within natural landscapes. Robert Smithson's *Spiral Jetty*, constructed in 1970 on the Great Salt Lake in Utah and Nancy's Holt's massive concrete *Sun Tunnels*, erected between 1973 and 1976 in Utah's Great Basin, are just a few of the most iconic Land Art creations, enduring monuments to the sacred partnership of nature and human will and imagination. In 1977, the artist Walter De Maria built his immersive installation *Lightning Field* in the deserts of western New

Daniel Buren · *Catch as catch can: work in situ* · France 2014 French sculptor Buren created the kaleido-scopic, rainbow mirrored exhibition at the Baltic Center for Contemporary Art in Gateshead, United

Kingdom. The artist designed the exhibit to respond directly to the space, allowing a subjective experience based on time of day and positioning within the room.

Noah Purifoy · *Outdoor Desert Art Museum* · United States · 1989 Using art to provoke change, Watts Towers Art Center co-founder and assemblage artist Purifoy, created more than a hundred works of art on over ten acres of land in Joshua Tree.

Lukas Kühne · *Tvísöngur Soundsculpture* · Germany 2012 Nestled in the dramatic mountainside of Seydisfjordur, Iceland, German artist Lukas Kühne designed the sculpture to be site-specific for the purpose of solitude, space, and sound frequency.

Mexico, erecting 400 polished steel poles in a careful grid, in the hopes of attracting lightning bolts and capturing the brilliant collision between land and storm-filled skies.

That same year, the prolific artist James Turrell began construction on perhaps his most epic undertaking, *The Roden Crater*, a still ongoing immersive artwork built within a volcanic cinder cone rising up from the Painted Desert of Arizona. Still a work-in-progress, the immense installation features various rooms carved from crater's crust, including an "observatory" for experiencing shifts of sunlight, sky, and the movement of the celestial spheres. Another long-term project is by the American artist Michael Heizer, who created a monumental complex in the Nevada desert, entitled, *City*. Breaking ground in 1970, the installation was finally opened to the public in 2022 and is considered one of the most ambitious Land Art projects ever undertaken.

In 1982, the artist Agnes Denes created what is perhaps the most seminal Land Art piece, entitled, *Wheatfield—A Confrontation*, which transformed a two-acre vacant lot in downtown Manhattan into a vast field of wheat. Over a period of four months, with the help of volunteers, she cleared the rubble-strewn field, spread 200 truckloads of soil, planted a field of golden wheat, tended it, and finally harvested it. The project saw the artist radically shift a segment of the city into a rural environment, and eventually feed it back into the urban community. The harvested grain traveled to 28 cities worldwide in, "The International Art Show for the End of World Hunger" and was symbolically planted around the globe.

The Minimalist artist Donald Judd often integrated his work into the outdoor landscape and in the 1970s, moved from New York City to the small town of Marfa, Texas, seeking a more expansive and secluded environment to create and display his artwork. He was drawn to the vast deserts and clear light of West Texas, which he felt provided an ideal setting for his sculptures. Judd acquired a large property in Texas where he installed permanent outdoor artwork and his presence in Marfa eventually attracted other artists, curators, and collectors to the town, sparking a cultural renaissance and establishing Marfa as an unexpected international art destination. In 2003, the gallery and exhibition space Ballroom Marfa also opened in Marfa, founded for the development and presentation of contemporary visual arts, music, and film. Hosting exhibitions, performances, film screenings and artist residencies, Ballroom's focus is showcasing contemporary works while engaging with the local community and integrating artwork into the distinct natural landscapes of the region.

Evolving alongside Land Art, the Light and Space Movement is another art genre that alters the viewer's perception and experience of space, using elements such as light and transparent, translucent, or reflective materials. Originating in Southern California in the 1960s, Light and Space artists created works that required viewers to engage with their surroundings in a more conscious way, creating deeply moving, deeply immersive experiences. Artists such as Robert Irwin and Doug Wheeler created sculpture and installation art by manipulating light and shadow to transform the viewer's perception of space. Larry Bell, another prominent Light and Space artist, is known for his glass cubes and large-scale glass installations that explore the relationship between the object and its environment. Lita Albuquerque is one of the most prolific artists emerging from both movements of the era and has created numerous site-specific installations all over the world, as well as paintings, immersive films, and performances. Her most recent work explores, as she explained in a 2022 interview, "the idea of a universal language that is at once cosmic and earthly based: life, planets, and elements, are formed through the explosion of supernovas; the gold used in religious artifacts or in wedding rings is formed through such cosmic forces (as are we)."

Throughout the last century and into the new, the emergence of environmental and immersive works has ignited an entirely unprecedented way of experiencing both art and space—with the viewer as participant, the land as gallery. Yoko Ono's, *The Wish Tree*, created in 1996, is one example, an interactive installation that invites visitors to make a wish and tie it to a branch of a living tree. Her *Sky Ladders*, built in 1997, consisted of a set of ladders reaching up towards the sky. More recently, the American artist Lauren Halsey, known for her large-scale installations and sculptures, created a radically contemporary take on an ancient Egyptian temple, high on the roof of the Metropolitan

Museum of Art. Entitled, *eastside of south central los angeles hieroglyph prototype architecture (I)*, the work incorporated classic pharaonic architecture alongside elements found within the urban landscapes of the artist's home of South-Central Los Angeles.

These varied expressions of art, some ephemeral, some permanent, some integrated into nature, others installed in urban landscapes, are in their own unique ways, sacred sites, meant to be worshipped and admired, meant to evoke feelings, reaction, and action. They remind us to be present and to be reverent. We are transformed as we bear witness to work like the Chinese artist and activist Ai Weiwei's fleeting fireworks pieces or Simone Leigh's monumental sculpture *Brick House*, which sits like a sentinel on the High Line in New York City. We are ignited by the rawness of art which incorporates the body and earth, that immerses us in emotion.

Judy Chicago's site-specific installations are another example of art which resonates with sacredness, such as in her iconic, *Smoke Bodies* Series, which features nude women, painted and powerful, posed amid clouds of colored smoke, standing strong against bright blue sky, and stark desert landscapes. Hugely prolific, Chicago's ongoing photography, sculpture and installation exhibitions explore the evolution of feminine archetypes and often focus on immersive interactions within natural environments. The artist has famously explained of her work, "I am trying to make art that relates to the deepest and most mythic concerns of humankind."

Andy Goldsworthy · *Still from Leaning into the Wind* **England** · **2017** Artist Andy Goldsworthy stars in the documentary on his life, exploring his home environment, self, and the impact of his art on the Scottish landscape, cities, and his own body.

(following, left) Andy Goldsworthy · *Le Vieil Esclangon from Refuge d'Art* · England · 2020 An extensive hike in the French Alps designed by the British artist Andy Goldsworthy in partnership with the Musée Gassendi and the National Natural Geology Reserve of Haute-Provence, takes you on a ninety-three-mile hike through sculptured landscapes, taking ten days to traverse.

(following, right) Deming King Harriman · *Amethyst Gateway* · United States · 2022 Colorfully contrasted, the cosmic collage is part of the celestial realms series by mixed media artist, Harriman, who explores the archetypes and symbolism of mythology, legend, and folklore.

Christo and Jeanne-Claude · *Wrapped Monument to Leonardo* Bulgaria/Morocco 1970 Monuments to the king of Italy Vittorio Emanuele II and Leonardo da Vinci, were wrapped with polypropylene fabric and red polypropylene rope by the artists in Milan, Italy.

(opposite, top) Yayoi Kusama · *Yellow Pumpkin* Japan · 1994 On a pier jutting out to sea on Naoshima island sits Yayoi Kusama's giant gourd. She writes of the project, "I would confront the spirit of the pumpkin. Forgetting everything else and concentrating my mind entirely on the form before me."

(opposite, bottom) Torkwase Dyson · *Liquid A Place* · United States · 2023 With the idea that we are water, and we blend with all bodies of water around us, Dyson invites viewers of the sculpture to consider our interconnectedness with life and memory.

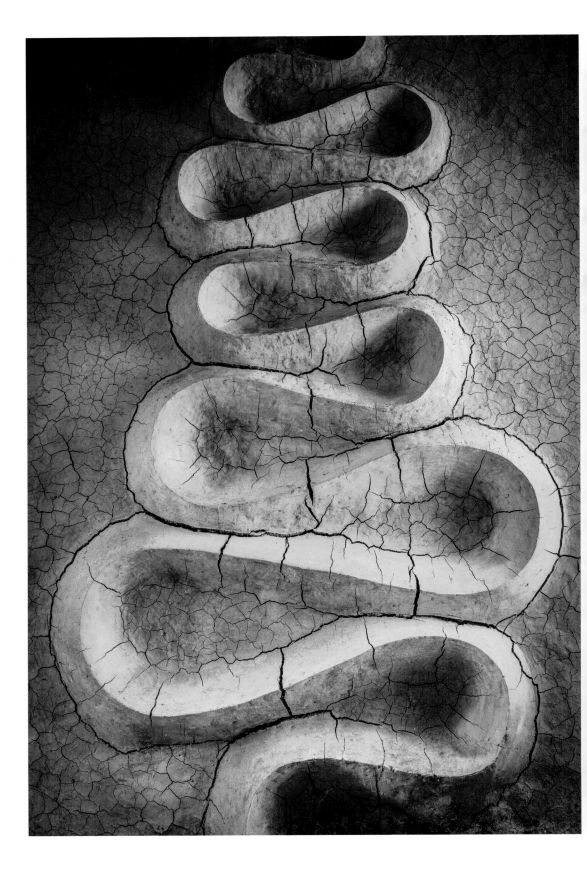

Agnes Pelton · *Resurgence*
United States · 1938
Soft and dreamy,
a point of transcendent
abstraction rises from
a frozen surface with
a focused trajectory
from the known to
the unknown. Pelton's
ethereal oil on canvas
expresses her under-
standing of such spiri-
tual truths that lead to
illumination.

Brice Bischoff · *Bronson Caves #11 and #12*
United States · 2010 Using a photographic
method of long-exposure on sheets of colored
paper which transformed into rainbow forms the

meditation and movement by the artist and inspired
by the cinematic history in the Los Angeles Bronson
cave, the images glisten with an ethereally cosmic
effervescence.

(previous pages) Fabrice Monteiro *Deforestation from The Prophecy* · Senegal 2015 To awaken collective consciousness to the environmental damage occurring in West Africa, Monteiro creates characters made of the destructive garbage on dry landscapes. His goal is to deliver the message through art across all cultures and continents.

Lucien Shapiro · *Final Fear Burn and Ceremony* United States · 2016 Of his performance art, like collecting fears in a 42-city tour then ritualistically burning them, Shapiro says, "Dancing between life and death, my art is rife with found objects, textures, cast forms, manipulations, and raw substances. Treating forgotten objects and memories as treasure, I create a kingdom under which new life is born through sculpture."

Chiharu Shiota · *I hope* · Japan · 2021 Japanese artist Shiota created a space to inspire us to believe again, as an immersive installation. Using thousands of letters sent to her from people around the world, sharing their hopes for the future, she wove the hopes together in scarlet threads.

Judy Chicago · *Multi-Color Atmosphere from the On Fire Suite* · United States · 1970 Feminizing the atmosphere of the male-dominated art scene was the intent behind Judy Chicago's site-specific fireworks performances around California in the seventies.

Paula Duró · *El Misterio de las Flores* · Argentina 2021 The Mystery of Flowers brings together the mysticism of nature and the interconnectedness between humans and the earth. Argentine artist, Duró, explores the balance of light and darkness in her art, in an effort to encourage rediscovery of the sacred unity we have with all things.

Betye Saar · *Legends in Blue* · United States 2020 American assemblage artist Betye Saar draws on spirituality and the use of found objects to produce her prolific and diverse creative explorations.

Yoko Ono · *Half-A-Room* · Japan · 1967 Japanese
artist and musician Yoko Ono sits in her installation
of a painted white, half bedroom entitled 'Half-A-
Room', part of her avant-garde 'Half-A-Wind Show'
exhibition at the Lisson Gallery in London in '67.

(following) Robert Smithson · *Spiral Jetty* · United
States · 1970 Constructed of over six thousand tons
of rock and sand, the massive manmade jetty off
the shore of Salt Lake in Utah, was built with the
intention of disintegration. It slowly erodes based on
the many changes of the earth, time, and climate.

**Alice Aycock · *Maze*
United States · 1972**
Prolific sculptor, Aycock often uses steel as her medium in constructing large scale installations which often appear to transcend the laws of gravity in somewhat mundane public spaces, landscapes, and institutions.

**Richard Long · *Dusty Boots Line, The Sahara*
England · 1988**
Described by the artist as "going nowhere," lines are formed on the ground by walking back and forth over and over again with a purposeless purpose and mindful beauty of walking for its own sake. This land art created in the desert of Algeria.

(opposite, top) Zhang Huan · *Three Legged Buddha*
China · 2007 Weighing over twelve tons, the giant copper and steel sculpture in Storm King outdoor museum in Hudson Valley, was conceived through the artist's viewpoint that our modernity is continually revitalized through an engagement with the past.

(opposite, bottom) Bruno Nasatti · *Louise Bourgeois's Maman* · Italy · 2012 Sculptor Bourgeois, built Maman to represent her mother's strength and protection. Standing over thirty feet high, this installation part of the Guggenheim Museum Bilbao.

477

Rachel Whiteread
Ghost · England · 1990
Made by filling a
room in a Victorian
home with concrete to
cast a mold of all the
cracks, crevices and
intricate details of the
walls and windows, the
artist's work typifies her
transformative ability to
turn everyday objects
and settings into ghostly
imprints infused with
memories of the past.

Elmgreen & Dragset
Prada Marfa
Denmark/Norway
2005 *Prada Marfa* is
a site specific, perma-
nent land art project
by artists Elmgreen &
Dragset, commissioned
by Art Production Fund
and Ballroom Marfa.
Modeled after a Prada
boutique, the sculpture
houses luxury goods
from the brand's fall
2005 collection of bags
and shoes.

Jonah Freeman and Justin Lowe · *Hello Meth Lab In The Sun* · United States · 2008 As a collaborative team, Freeman and Lowe actualize fictional,
cultural situations into visual spaces by creating
architectural and immersive installations in
site-specific locations. The dystopian drug lab
disaster presents audiences an up-close view
of what can only be imagined.

478

(following pages)
Liza Lou · *Kitchen*
United States · 1991-96
Five years in the making,
the full scale, highly
detailed kitchen replica
fashioned with papi-
er-mâché and mosaic
beadwork, is described
by Lou as an argument
for the dignity of labor.
Traditionally a woman's
domain, *Kitchen* com-
ments on the gender
roles of American life.

Jeanne K. Simmons · *Extensions* · United States
2020 As an extension of herself, her hair, her
nervous system, and nature, in this series the artist
demonstrates the unbreakable bond we have with
the natural world by literally braiding the model's
hair with the grass of the earth.

Mark di Suvero · *Hugs* · United States · 2011
Allowing viewers to engage in a kinesthetic experience, the massive three-legged installation in New
York is art for all people without the trappings of
museum hierarchy.

Michael Heizer · *City*
United States · 1972
Artist Michael Heizer
built the mile and a half
long sculpture in the
Nevada desert based
on ancient ritual cities.
Made from rock, sand
and concrete mined
onsite, the monumental
structure was made to
destroy. Then, President
Obama declared seven
hundred and four thou-
sand acres of pristine
wilderness surrounding
the work, a national
monument, thus pre-
serving it.

Laura Bon and
Metabolic Studio
Underland · United
States · 2021 Using
the natural resources
of a place's environ-
ment, the foundation
of the L.A. River is
perforated to allow an
alternative flow route
for water that would
normally flush out to
sea. The redirection will
pass through a native
wetland treatment, and
eventually be distributed
to local parks including
the 52-acre L.A. State
Historic Park.

(opposite) Marianne Gast · *Dancers from Ballet
Experimental de El Eco* · Germany · 1953 Using
public space as her medium, Gast sparked contro-
versy during cultural and political transformation,
helping to define a modernized Mexican state of
liberated thinking. She used "emotional

architecture" in his public performances, to spiritually articulate her ideas. Here she photographs
dancers (one of whom is Walter Nicks) in front of
La Serpiente—a sculpture by her husband Mexican
artist Mathias Goeritz.

Olafur Eliasson · *The Weather Project* · Iceland/ Denmark · 2003 In the site-specific installation, an artificially devised sun is formed using mirrors, lights, and mist.

Ai WeiWei · *Gilded Cage* · China · 2017 To bring awareness to the refugee urgency, Ai builds a giant bird cage and other symbolic installations in the southeast corner of Central Park in New York City, and in other conspicuous locations around the metro area.

Barbara Kasten
Architectural Site 17
United States · 1988
The complex and elaborate task of photography as assemblage art from materials including painted wood, plaster, mirrors, screens, and fibers, defines the works of Kasten, who used light and mirrors to affect form and space within the Richard Meier designed building.

Various · *The Real Unreal* · United States 2023 Originally conceived and realized in Santa Fe, New Mexico, the fourth location of Meow Wolf—an immersive art installation which is a whole museum in itself—opens in Texas. With over thirty rooms of detailed psychedelic and surreal art to explore, visitors are transported through portal after portal of imaginative amazement.

Dan Flavin · *Untitled (for Leo Castelli at his Gallery's 30th Anniversary)* · United States · 1989 Having discovered, supported, and promoted many pop art icons, like Andy Warhol, Dan Flavin, Roy Lichtenstein, and Jasper Johns, in their early phases, Leo Castelli is honored in the lit piece.

Ugo Rondinone · *Seven Magic Mountains* · Switzerland
2016 Swiss artist Rondinone's large-scale site-specific public art installation is a creative expression of
human presence in the desert, punctuating the
Mojave with a poetic burst of form and color.

Chris Holmes · *The Journey Within* · United States
2024 To elicit psychedelic perception of immersion
into sound and light, DJ Holmes creates happen-
ings that stimulate the body's ability to enter trance-
like states.

Anila Quayyum Agha · *Intersections* · Pakistan/
United States · 2013 Hung from the ceiling, the
steel structure is perforated with geometric and
floral design and illuminated from within to create
shadows in every direction, including the visitors
to the space.

(following) Barry William Hale · *Arcanorum 231*
Australia · 2021–23 The VR temple was inspired by
Aleister Crowley's magical work *Liber Arcanorum*.
Featuring Hale's art and the myth of *The Crata
Repoa*, users can engage in invocations, drumming,
and chanting to invoke the tarot spirits Crowley's text.

(following)
Doug Aitken · *Mirage*
United States · 2017
Composed of mirrored surface, the site-specific installation takes the form of a ranch-style home in the California desert. It reflects the nature that surrounds it, therefore becomes one with the landscape, invoking a unique interpretation in each who views it.

Kathryn Garcia · *Film still from 'She changes everything She touches, and everything She touches changes'* · Ibiza/United States · 2023 The artist kneels on the shore just off the vortex island of Es Vedra in Spain in the film still. Tanit, the Phoenician Goddess is superimposed over the film, showcasing the artist's connection to this deity.

Nugzar Manjaparashvili · *Peace* Georgia · 1970s Resembling a reclined Buddha, the sculpture was erected in 1970 in Nukriani. As a state-commissioned monument, it was built to commemorate Georgia's participation in the Second World War.

(opposite) Elena Stonaker · *Big Mama from 'In Snake's Belly' installation* · United States · 2019 An artist and designer whose work is inspired by myths and storytelling, Stonaker's soft-sculptures reference, as the artist explains, "the goddess figure, mother figure. I make them in order to make us feel small, so we can feel how we did when we were children, when we were naturally full of awe."

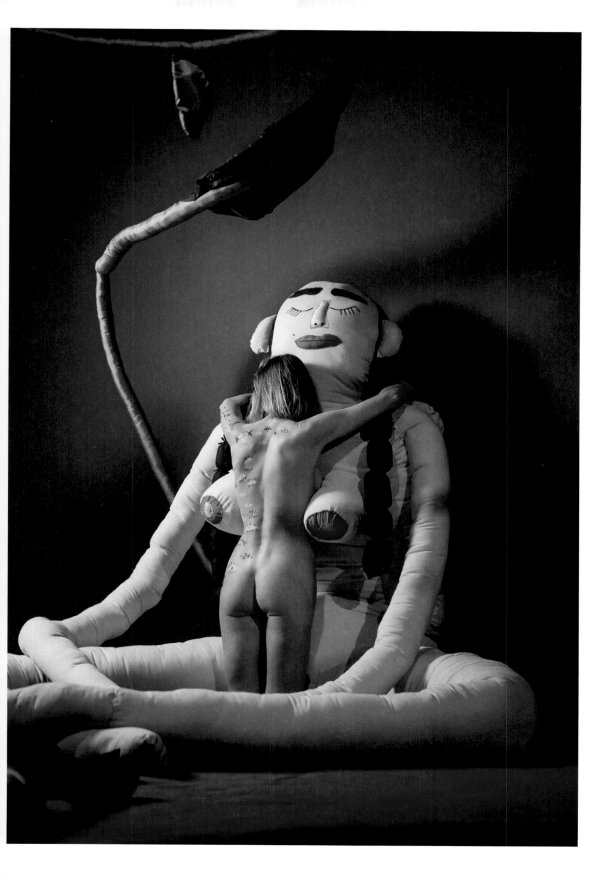

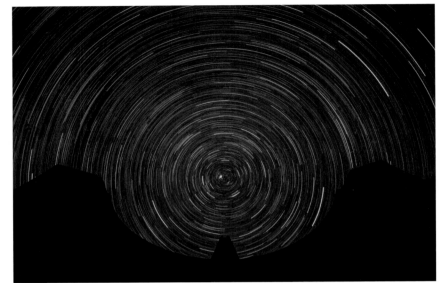

(previous) Nancy Holt *Sun Tunnels* · United States · 1973–76 Four concrete tubes lay in the remote Great Basin Desert of Utah, with perfectly drilled holes which filter in light to cast constellations on the interior tubes. To capture the close-up cosmic conditions provides a literal experience of 'as above, so below.'

Charles Ross · *Star Axis: Star Tunnel* United States **Ongoing** Conceived in 1971, the eleven-story high by 160 meter across earth/sky sculpture is nearing completion in the remote New Mexico desert. *Star Axis* is an earthwork built to observe the stars. Its architectonic geometry is precisely determined by earth-to-star alignments so they can be experienced in physical form and human scale.

Walter De Maria · *The Lightning Field* · United States · 1977 On a site chosen for its isolation and far distance from human interaction, the land art installation consisting of four-hundred-pointed, stainless-steel poles is precisely positioned to create a grid within which visitors are encouraged to walk through. It is considered a minimalist masterpiece. No phones, cameras or cars are allowed to this space of reflection and disconnection from the information age.

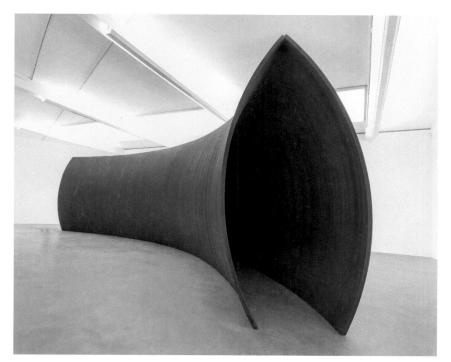

(opposite, top) Jim Denevan · *Lake Baikal, Siberia* · United States 2010 Designed according to the Fibonacci sequence, and world's largest single art piece-lay on a frozen lake in Siberia. Like all of his temporary land art, the enormous Lake Baikal drawing dissolved after a few months, due to weather conditions.

(opposite, bottom) Andrew Rogers · *Knot* Australia · 2008 Hundreds of Nepalese people assisted Rogers in his large-scale land art in Pokhara. Called the "Rhythms of Life" project, his landscape forms currently consist of 51 massive earth drawings made with stones. The endless knot symbolizes the endless cycle of life and rebirth within Tibetan Buddhism.

Richard Serra *Backdoor Pipeline* United States · 2010 The cave-like and confining shape of the bent steel sculpture in London's Gagosian Gallery is meant to be walked through. It leads visitors into complete darkness then back into light.

(previous, right top)
Ensamble Studio
(Antón García-Abril
and Débora Mesa)
Inverted Portal · Spain
2016 The team at
Ensamble Studio blur
the lines between
land, art, architecture,
structure, and sculpture.
Using found materials,
their work transcends
architectural boundaries
and time periods to
produce a pure and
direct emotional impact.

Maya Lin · *Storm King
Wavefield* · United
States · 2009 On
eleven acres in New
Windsor, New York,
Maya Lin created the
four-acre set of waves
on an ocean of green,
designed in the same
scale as actual waves
that allow a viewer to
experience a feeling
of being at sea.

Agnes Denes · *Wheatfield—A Confrontation: Battery Park Landfill* · United States · 1982 On a downtown Manhattan landfill site, Denes planted a field of grain, by hand, as a symbol of food, energy, commerce, world trade, and economics, and to highlight mismanagement, waste, world hunger and ecological issues.

Wheatfield—A Confrontation, *took place at the Battery Park Landfill, in downtown Manhattan. I did the project in 1982, but it gained added poignancy after the 9/11 disaster at the same site where the Wheatfield had been. My decision to plant a wheatfield in Manhattan instead of designing just another public sculpture grew out of a long-standing concern and need to call attention to our misplaced priorities and deteriorating human values. Manhattan is the richest, most professional, most congested, and without a doubt, most fascinating island in the world. To attempt to plant, sustain, and harvest two acres of wheat here, wasting valuable real estate, obstructing the machinery by going against the system, was an effrontery that made it the powerful paradox I had sought for the calling to account. Placing it at the foot of the World Trade Center, a block from Wall Street, facing the Statue of Liberty, was to be a careful reminder of what this land had stood for and hopefully still does. Wheatfield was a symbol, a universal concept. It represented food, energy, commerce, world trade, economics. It referred to mismanagement, waste, world hunger, and ecological concerns. It was an intrusion into the Citadel, a confrontation of High Civilization. Then again, it was also Shangri-la, a small paradise, one's childhood, a hot summer afternoon in the country, peace, forgotten values, simple pleasures. The idea of a wheatfield is quite simple. One penetrates the soil, places one's seed of concept, and allows it to grow, expand, and bear fruit. That is what creation and life is all about. It's all so simple, yet we tend to forget basic processes. What was different about this wheatfield was that the soil was not rich loam, but dirty landfill filled with rusty metals, boulders, old tires, and overcoats. It was not farmland but an extension of the congested downtown of a metropolis where dangerous crosswinds blew, traffic snarled, and every inch was precious reality. The absurdity of it all, the risks we took, and the hardships we endured were all part of the basic concept. Digging deep is what art is all about.*

— AGNES DENES, Multimedia Artist, 2024

(opposite) Simon
Rodia · *Watts Towers*
**Italy/United States
1921–65** Standing as
a symbol of freedom,
creativity, and power
for social change and
justice, the Watts Towers
is a folk-art assemblage
built by Simon Rodia
in the Watts neighbor-
hood in Los Angeles,
California.

Courtney Alexander
God Is · **United States
2023** Inspired by
Central African mas-
querades, the artist
ritualizes the higher
spirit of self, creating
a space for audiences
to make offerings to
the divinity of self-love.
Offerings made to Alex-
ander are then offered
to a river in a circular
flow of love and giving.

Judy Chicago
Immolation IV
United States · 1972
From her *Woman and
Smoke* series, Faith
Wilding models the
ritual of the outmoded
Indian practice called
sati in which a widower
sacrifices herself by
setting herself on fire
on the funeral pyre of
her husband.

FOR THE SEEKERS

A Final Note on the Library of Esoterica

The Library of Esoterica explores the expansive visual history of the arcane, showcasing artwork birthed through the expressions of a wide variety of traditions and rituals. The intent of this series is to offer inclusive, introductory overviews to these ancient rituals and to explore their complex symbolism objectively, rather than dogmatically.

In doing so, the aspiration is to draw back the veil to reveal a deeper appreciation of these valuable tools of the psyche. Esoteric knowledge offers powerful methods for self-exploration and meditation. These magickal practices have developed over centuries in order to allow for a further understanding of the inner world.

The goal of this series is to present condensed summaries of these ancient systems and from there, encourage readers to further explore the rituals, ceremonies, and sacred philosophies of various global cultures. The task is to inspire readers to seek out knowledge, to study the teachings of scholars past and present, who have dedicated themselves to the development and preservation of these ancient arts.

The hope is that *The Library of Esoterica* emboldens readers to begin their own journey down into the dark halls of the arcane, to pull the dusty tomes from the shelves, to take the timeworn cards from the satchel and spread them across the silks, to look up to the sky and read meaning in the movement of the stars.

As the author, teacher, and archivist Manly P. Hall stated so eloquently in his masterwork, *The Secret Teachings of All Ages*, "To live in the world without becoming aware of the meaning of the world is like wandering about in a great library without touching the books." Later, in this indispensable and exhaustive overview of the world's esoteric teachings, Hall exclaims, "Only transcendental philosophy knows the path. Only the illumined reason can carry the understanding part of man upward to the light. Only philosophy can teach man to be born well, to live well, to die well, and in perfect measure, be born again. Into this band of the elect, those who have chosen the life of knowledge, of virtue, and of utility, the philosophers of the ages invite, YOU."

(previous)
Lita Albuquerque
Still from 'Liquid Light'
United States · 2018
In a still from Albuquerque's experimental art film, Director of Photography David McFarland captures Albuquerque's iconic female astronaut character. In the film, the character seeks to reconnect us with our cosmic origins and knowledge but has difficulty communicating the concepts of peace and harmony to earth's inhabitants due to the current state of world affairs.

Niki de Saint Phalle · *SHE—A Cathedral* · France/ United States · 1966 Taking up the entire space in the center of the Moderna Museet Museum in Stockholm, Sweden, Feminist artist Niki de Saint Phalle's giant female body sculpture could be entered through the figure's vagina, into the inner space of her corporeal reality. Serving to disrupt the power dynamics, gender and cultural rules and norms, the installation shifted perspectives and paradigms, photographed here by Hans Hammarskiöld.

BIBLIOGRAPHY

Albuquerque, Lita, Selma Holo, Roger F. Malina, David B. Walker, William L. Fox, Ann M. Wolfe, Jean de Pomereu, and Brad Bartlett. Lita Albuquerque: Stellar Axis. New York: Skira Rizzoli, 2014.

Alvarez, Melissa. Earth frequency: Sacred sites, Vortexes, Earth Chakras, and other transformational places. Woodbury, MN: Llewellyn Publications, 2019.

Arnold, Leigh A., Lita Albuquerque, Alice Aycock, Beverly Buchanan, Agnes Denes, Maren Hassinger, Nancy Holt, et al. Groundswell: Women of land art. Dallas, TX: Nasher Sculpture Center, 2023.

Blavatsky, H. P. The land of the gods: The long-hidden story of visiting the masters of wisdom in Shambhala. New York NY: Radiant Books, 2022.

Campbell, Joseph, and Diane K. Osbon. A Joseph Campbell Companion: Reflections on the art of living. New York, NY: HarperPerennial, 1998.

Campbell, Joseph, and Nancy Allison. The ecstasy of being: Mythology and dance. Novato, CA: New World Library, 2023.

Campbell, Joseph, and Nancy Allison. The ecstasy of being: Mythology and dance. Novato, CA: New World Library, 2023.

Derrick, Martin. Unforgettable ancient sites: Mysterious sites, temple complexes, ancient architecture. New York, NY: Chartwell Books, an imprint of The Quarto Group, 2018.

Gimbutas, Marija AlseikaitE. The language of the goddess: Unearthing the. San Francisco: Harper & Row, 1989.

Gimbutas, Marija. The Civilization of the Goddess. HarperCollins Publishers, n.d.

Gray, Martin. Secret sacred sites. Versailles: Jonglez publishing, 2023.

Iyer, Pico. A beginner's guide to japan: Observations and provocations. New York: Vintage Departures, 2020.

IYER, PICO. Half known life: In search of paradise. NEW YORK: RIVERHEAD BOOKS, 2024.

Jones, Wilson Mark. Origins of classical architecture: Temples, orders and gifts to the gods in Ancient Greece. New Haven: Yale University Press, 2014.

Kahn, Lloyd, and Bob Easton. Shelter. Bolinas, CA: Shelter Publications, Inc, 2015.

Myerson, Joel. Transcendentalism: A reader. Oxford: Oxford University Press, 2000.

PIETSCH, BERNARD I. Written in stone and space: The invisible language of ancient architecture. S.l.: BOOKBABY, 2023.

Saint-Phalle, Niki de, and Giulio Pietromarchi. The tarot garden. Salenstein, SW: Benteli, 2017.

Tiberghien, Gilles A. Land art. London: Art Data, 1995.

Whitman, Walt, and Malcolm Cowley. The complete poetry and prose of Walt Whitman as prepared by him for the deathbed edition: Two volumes in one. Garden City, N.Y: Garden City Books, 1954.

IMAGE CREDITS

258. Herefordshire Libraries: 9, 40. Herzog August Bibliothek Wolfenbuettel: Cod. Guelf. 74.1 Aug. 2°, folio 25r: 45. Photograph by Michael P. Smith © The Historic New Orleans Collection, 2007.0103.3.30: 109. © Holt/Smithson Foundation and Dia Art Foundation/ARS, New York: 474, 498. The Hopper Art Trust: 418. John Lindquist Photograph. © Houghton Library, Harvard University: 122. Imogen Cunningham Trust: 148. Jason Taellious: 454. Jeaneen Lund: 78. Jeanne K Simmons: 480. Jerry de Wilde: 303, 336, 390. Jim Denevan (artist)/Peter Hinson (photographer): 501. Joyce Lee: 164. Kathryn Garcia: 494. Kenro Izu: 293. Nicholas Kahn & Richard Selesnick: 112. Photo Lance Gerber: 463, 496. Lauren Bon and Metabolic Studio. David Baine photograph: 485. © Lauren Halsey. Courtesy of the artist; David Kordansky Gallery, Los Angeles/New York. Photo by Hyla Skopitz, courtesy of the Metropolitan Museum of Art, New York: 55. Lawrence Schiller: 400. © Leslie Williamson: 383. Library of Congress: 283; /Prints and Photographs Division Washington, D.C. 20540: 44. Lisson Gallery/Photo-souvenir: Daniel Buren, Catch as Catch Can, work in situ, Baltic Center for Contemporary Art, Gateshead, 2014. Détail © Daniel Buren: 457. Lita Albuquerque, courtesy of the artist /film still by Hesham Alsaifi and Nicole McDonald: 7; /photo by Lance Gerber: 59; /photo by Michael Lights: 137. Liza Lou/Collection Whitney Museum of American Art, New York, NY: 482. Los Angeles Public Library, Made accessible through a grant from the John Randolph Haynes and Dora Haynes Foundation: 433. Louvre Abu Dhabi + Giuseppe Penone Studio © Department of Culture and Tourism – Abu Dhabi / Photo Roland Halbe: 453. Lucien Shapiro: 470. Lyn Winter: 463, 496, 591. Magda Wosinska: 177. Magnum Photos/ Herbert List: 157. Photo © MAK / MAK – Museum of Applied Arts, Vienna: 353. Manzel Bowman: 276. Marcella Blood Estate: 115. Maria Austria Institute + Caption Gallery: 248. Maria Filopoulou: 84. Marina Abramovic Courtesy of Mark di Suvero and Spacetime C.C./Photo Steven Probert: 481. Mary Evans Picture Library © Ashmolean Museum: 255. © Massimo Listri: 446. Massimo Scolari: 349. Matthias Dengler: 391. Maximilien Bruggmann: 224, 232. ©

Maya Lin Studio: 504. Lawren S. Harris (1885– 1970), Mount Robson c. 1929, oil on canvas, 128.3 x 152.4 cm, Purchase 1979, McMichael Canadian Art Collection 1979.20 © Family of Lawren S. Harris: 92. Md. Ahsanul Haque Nayem: 37. Meagan Boyd: 142. Michael Carter: 176. Michael Whelan: 362. Michal Klajban: 172. Michael T. Bies: 233. © Mœbius Production – Jean Giraud Mœbius: 352. Mohammadreza Domiriganji: 35, 299. Courtesy Monica Sjöö Estate and Alison Jacques, London © Monica Sjöö Estate, Photo: Krister Hägglund: 152. Munson-Williams-Proctor Institute of Art: 99. Musée Picasso, Paris: 170. Museum of Performance + Design/Anna Halprin Collection: 126. Myriam Wares: 13. Nadia Waheed: 42. Collection Nationaal Museum van Wereldculturen (Museum Volkenkunde, Leiden): 135. The National Gallery, London, Picture Library: 88, 445. KB National Library of the Netherlands, The Hague: 180. National Library of Wales: 193. New York Public Library: 89. Nicolas Peña: 21. Nicole Geri: 307. Courtesy Pace Gallery: 476, 504. Paula Duró: 472. Pedro Szekely: 16. Peter Granser/laif from his book 'El Alto' by Edition Taube: 385. Philosophical Research Society: 311, 428. Photofest/HBO: 356; /Warner Bros.: 356, 363. © Pierre et Gilles: Mercure, Enzo junior, 2001: 178. Posteritati: 266. Courtesy Public Art Fund, NY/ Courtesy of Ai Weiwei Studio/ Frahm & Frahm / Photo: Liz Ligon: 487. Redux Pictures: 380. Rijksmuseum: 301. © IMEC, Fonds MCC, Dist. RMN-Grand Palais/Gisèle Freund: 417. Courtesy of the artist and Roberts Projects, Los Angeles, California. Photo: Alan Shaffer: 472. Royal Collection Trust/© His Majesty King Charles III 2023: 261. Courtesy of Rule Gallery, Drop City Archive: 399. Sander Berg: 312. Scala, Florence/Adagp Images, Paris: 154; / Christie's Images, London: 104; /Photo Austrian Archives: 148. Shutterstock/Dmitri Kessel/The LIFE Picture Collection: 296; /Yale Joel/The LIFE Picture Collection: 382. ©The Dome at Sir John Soane's Museum, London. Photo by Gareth Gardner: 423. South Asian Art Gallery: 136. © Archive Szukalski: 56, 358. The State Hermitage Museum, St Petersburg, photo by Vladimir Terebenin: 128. Photo Stefano Perego: 494. Stephanie Law: 355. © The Steven Arnold Museum and Archives: 408. Stephen

For those seeking to explore the history, art, and architecture of sacred spaces, we encourage everyone to support the work of all the wonderful artists and interviewees included in this volume. The following is a brief list of individuals and institutions that offer invaluable information through their print and digital media.

INDIVIDUALS

Lita Albuquerque, Agnes Denes, Fairfax Dorn, Sarah Drew, Isis Indriya, Virginia Lebermann, Santosh Khalsa

WEBSITES / PODCASTS / MEDIA

Conscious Cities, Cultivating Place, Double Blind, Weird Walk, Shelter Publications, Whole Earth Catalogue

INSTITUTIONS

Arcosanti, Ballroom Marfa, Beinecke Rare Book and Manuscript Library, The British Library, The British Museum, Dublab, Esalen Institute, Creative Folkestone/Prospect Cottage, CoSM/Chapel of Sacred Mirrors, Fascinated by Everything, The Getty Research Institute, The Henry Miller Library, The Huntington Library, Art Museum and Gardens, The Krotona Institute of Theosophy, The Met, The Morgan Library, Namuna, NASA, The Opus Archives, Academy of Oracle Arts, Pacifica Institute, The Philosophical Research Society, Palma Colectiva, The Tarot Garden, Tuscany

Thank you to the artists, authors, publishers, and scholars kind enough to share their knowledge and passion with us and for the generous participation of the many unique voices that have offered wisdom through their insightful interviews. Thank you to Lita Albuquerque for her generosity and wisdom.

We are endlessly grateful to all those who have offered support, connections and encouragement throughout this project including Kelly Carmena of the Philosophical Research Society, Devon Deimler of the Opus Archives, Mark McNeill, Veronica Tsai and Emily Utne.

And finally, this book would not exist without the talent and dedication of Nic & J.B. Taylor and Lisa Doran, and the wisdom and encouragement of Kathrin Murr, Marion Boschka, David Kenzler, Mahros Allamezade, Andy Disl, and Benedikt Taschen.

— LOE SERIES EDITOR,
JESSICA HUNDLEY, 2024

IMPRINT

Edited by Jessica Hundley

Written by Jessica Hundley
Captions by Michelle Mae

Design by Thunderwing

Visual Research & Licensing by Lisa Doran

All images and quotations are © Copyright
their respective copyright owner. In case of
any inadvertent errors or omissions in credit,
please contact the publisher. Excerpts featured
throughout the book have been edited from
the publications cited. In some cases, they have
been slightly condensed or edited for clarity.

ISBN 978-3-8365-9060-0
Printed in Boznia-Herzegovina

© 2024 TASCHEN GmbH
Hohenzollernring 53, D-50672 Köln
www.taschen.com

(front cover) Apollo 8 Spacecraft · *Earth and Moon:
Earthrise* · Outer Space · 1968

(back cover) Caspar David Friedrich · *Wanderer
Above the Sea of Fog* · Germany · 1818